C000054142

The Bible Made Clear

For Bergl
with food wishes

David Winter

Abingdon 2010

The Bible

Made Clear
David Winter

Copyright © 2008 David Winter
This edition copyright © 2008 Lion Hudson

The author asserts the moral right
to be identified as the author of this work

A Lion Book
an imprint of
Lion Hudson plc
Wilkinson House, Jordan Hill Road,
Oxford OX2 8DR, England
www.lionhudson.com
ISBN 978 0 7459 5273 4 (UK)
ISBN 978 0 8254 6267 2 (US)

First published in 2004 as *Making Sense of the Bible*
This revised edition 2008
10 9 8 7 6 5 4 3 2 1 0

Distributed by:

UK: Marston Book Services, PO Box 269, Abingdon,
      Oxon, OX14 4YN
USA: Trafalgar Square Publishing, 814 N. Franklin Street,
      Chicago, IL 60610
USA: Christian Market: Kregel Publications, PO Box 2607,
      Grand Rapids, Michigan 49501

All rights reserved

Acknowledgments

Scripture quotations are taken from the New Revised
Standard Version published by HarperCollins Publishers,
copyright © 1989 by the Division of Christian Education
of the National Council of the Churches of Christ in the
USA, and are used by permission. All rights reserved.

A catalogue record for this book is available
from the British Library

Typeset in 10.5/14 IowanOldStyleBT
Printed and bound in China

Contents

Introduction

Perhaps this book needs a bit of explanation right at the start. It is intended for people who would, on the whole, on balance, and without wanting to get fanatical about it, like to read and make sense of the Bible – in other words, the 'rest of us', not people like this author, who has spent most of his working life reading the Bible and trying to persuade other people to do the same. It starts with the Bible's 'plot' (thus giving the story away right from the beginning) and ends with a kind of 'Reduced Bible' for those who would like to read the low-fat, high-protein abbreviated version.

In case you are baffled by the little numbers in brackets dotted about the book, these are references to books, chapters and verses of the Bible. It's not necessary to look them up, unless you want to check that I'm not trying to pull a fast one. They're there because you might at some point want to verify what I'm claiming from the actual text of the book. If you do, then the clue is as follows: the first thing given (unless it's already been mentioned) is the book of the Bible (see its index, at the front of most editions). The next figure is the chapter in that book, followed by a colon and the numbers of the verse or verses being referred to.

I apologize if all that sounds patronizing, but at least it may reassure some readers that I've tried not to take anything for granted – except two things, I suppose. The first is that you own, or can borrow, a copy of the Bible, preferably in a reliable modern version (I've used the New Revised Standard Version, but the New International Version or the Revised English Bible would do just as well). The second is that you have some level of motivation to tackle the most influential book in the history of world literature.

1

A Bird's Eye View: What's the Story?

A man and a woman fell into a muddy pit, from which there was no escape. They hollered and hollered for help, but no one came, until at last they heard footsteps. A bearded man looked over the edge. 'Dear me,' he said, 'You've fallen into the pit. Wait a minute, I've got something here that may help you.' He rummaged in a capacious pocket for a while, and then threw a slim book down to them. 'Here, read that.' And then he walked away, leaving them to pick the book out of the mud. Wiping it clean, they read the title: Ten Ways to Avoid Falling Down Pits. Not much help there, then. So they hollered some more.

Eventually, more footsteps approached. They shouted loudly, 'Help!' Another bearded man looked over the edge of the pit. 'Ah,' he said wisely. 'You've fallen into the pit, I see. Well, I've got news for you. Someone's coming to get you out.' With that he disappeared, but at least he had given them some hope. They sat and waited for this promised rescuer.

And waited, and waited. After what seemed an eternity, there were more footsteps. Again a face appeared at the top of the pit, but a younger one. A ladder was let down and the young man climbed down to stand in the mud alongside them. 'Right,' he said, 'I've come to get you out. Trust me, I know what I'm doing.' With that he grabbed the woman, slung her over his shoulder and carried her up the ladder, coming down to repeat the task with the man. They were profuse in their thanks, but then made to resume their original journey. 'Wait a minute,' said the young man. 'Can't have you falling down any more pits, can we? I'm coming with you for the rest of the journey.' So they set off, the three of them, leaving behind the darkness and slime and heading into what looked attractively like the rising sun.

A Book with a Story

At this point you may well be asking whether the publishers have got two different manuscripts muddled. On the contrary, that story – which could come from a child's adventure book, rather than one on reading the Bible – introduces the main argument of this chapter, because it offers in cartoon form a summary of the Bible's 'plot'. And one of the chief reasons people find the Bible a confusing, obscure and even irrelevant book is that they haven't realized that there is a plot, but read it as a disjointed thesaurus of wise sayings, sound advice and preposterous stories. Once you begin to fit the parts into the whole, it emerges as a coherent entity, a book, or collection of books, with something to say, with an argument to put across or a story to tell.

You've only got to open a Bible, or at least rifle through its pages, to see that it's not like most of the books we read. It doesn't have one author, but many authors. It's not one book but sixty-six. And it's almost impossible to put it into any recognizable literary category. Some of it is a chronicle of events. Some of it is poetry.

Job's Evil Dreams by William Blake, an illustration of the book of Job.

Some of it offers the reader wise sayings, or visions, or prophecies of the future. Some of the books are letters to various people, or groups of people. And four books describe themselves as 'Gospels' or 'Good News'. You may well find yourself asking what sort of a 'book' this one is.

A Hotchpotch?

I suspect that many people, knowing the Bible's reputation and influence on world thought, have picked it up and been put off to find that it isn't like other great and influential books, which have an author, a beginning, a middle and an end, and pursue one consistent line of argument all through. At first – and even second – glance the Bible looks like a hotchpotch, with no plot, no author, and no consistent argument running through its pages. For instance, those embarking on Genesis, its first book, will find a massive change of gear between the first eleven chapters and the twelfth. They might well then pursue a fairly clear chronicle of events until they get to Leviticus and find themselves in what reads like a directory of ritual practices. At this point, many would-be readers of the Bible give up in despair. How do you make sense of a book without argument or plot?

In fact, as I have tried to show, the Bible does have both an argument and a plot. It tells the story of the human race and its relationship with its Creator, but it tells it in many different 'voices': poetry, allegory, narrative, vision and teaching. Because it doesn't have one human author, but many, there is no coherent style; in fact, there is no distinctive language either. To readers of the Bible there may seem to be a common biblical style of language, but this has been created by the translators rather than the original writers. In fact, when people say that they love the 'language' of the Bible, they usually mean that they like the Tudor English of the Authorized Version. I doubt if they would find much literary merit in the letters of the apostle Paul, or the Gospel of Mark, or the book of Leviticus, if they read them in their original Greek or Hebrew.

Studying the Dead Sea Scrolls.

A Story to Tell

In truth, most of the original authors weren't much bothered about literary polish. They had a story to tell, or an experience to recount, or a vision to describe. As they were setting it down, it would never have occurred to them that one day their words would be incorporated in a large collection of books and published as 'The Bible'. They were contributing to an overall argument or plot, but as they wrote they could not possibly have known that. Their immediate goal was to set down what they had learned or experienced, believing that it added something to the sum total of human knowledge about God and his ways with us.

The plot, as it were, emerges from all of these varied experiences and accounts. However, it is a real one, and it is the main reason that the Bible has survived and been valued by Christians down the centuries. This book actually says something quite coherent, and even presents a universal argument, almost (if one can put it this way) by accident. Of course, believers don't see it as an accident, but as the work of divine providence – though it is not a prerequisite of Bible reading to accept that on trust.

At the risk of stating the obvious, the childish story with which I began this chapter relates to the great, seminal events of the Bible's narratives. There is the Fall – an explanation, probably in allegorical form, both for the presence of evil in the world and for the moral plight in which the human race finds itself. The man and the woman 'fell'. Making use of their divinely ordained gift of moral autonomy, or free will, they chose to ignore God's instructions and consequently ended up... well, stuck down a pit.

Then there is the large section of the Old Testament, the Hebrew Scriptures, which deals with the Law, summarized in the famous 'Ten Commandments'. These set out God's standards for his creation, standards that we are warned we flout at our peril. In the language of our cartoons, they 'stop us falling down pits' – but they came a bit late in the day for the first man and woman, known as Adam and Eve. However, it is also true that those same writings constantly remind us that God has not abandoned his children, but is seeking them and longing for their response to him in obedience and trust.

An Army of Visionaries

Then came the Prophets, that great army of visionaries who provide most of the second half of the Old Testament, men like Isaiah (possibly two, or even three men, in fact), Jeremiah, Ezekiel and a host more. These were people who somehow tapped into a vein of insight not open to most of us, to see greater truths and offer both warning and hope to their hearers. Though they spoke with human voices, their sayings are invariably prefixed with the words, 'Thus says the Lord.' They spoke, and they made promises; most of all, they promised that the God who had not forgotten his human creatures would one day send a rescuer or Saviour to put them on the right path again.

Moving on to the New Testament, we start with the Gospels – contemporary records or impressions of the life and teaching of Jesus, whom the authors regarded as precisely that promised Saviour. Their story is that he came to where we were, stuck in the pit of failure and fear, and by his life, death and resurrection lifted us to where God wants us to be – on a journey to him.

Lastly, there is the story of the new community that arose out of the life and teaching of Jesus, a community of people who have his Spirit living among them, guiding, strengthening and guarding them; as Jesus said, 'I am with you always.'

That, in a ludicrously brief and arbitrary summary, is the 'plot' of the Bible, a plot that emerges from the work of its forty or so authors writing an immensely varied collection of books. Holding that shape in mind enables a reader to see the various parts in the context of the whole, whereas often, too often, the Bible is read as a series of extracts quite unrelated to each other. So for many people the Bible is principally a work of literature, a classic, even, but really consisting of a collection of quotations. Some people know the 23rd Psalm, for instance ('The Lord is my shepherd'), while others would cite one or other of the sayings of Jesus: 'Blessed are the meek,' 'Turn the other cheek,' 'Love your enemies'. The Bible is seen as a kind of thesaurus of sayings and poetry, rather than the story of the human race in its search for God (and God in his search for us) which it claims to be.

Who's the Author?

Having said that, the question of authorship still remains. Symposia are seldom bestsellers, mainly because they lack the

The Synagogue of the Premishlan congregation at Bnei Brak, Israel. The rabbi is reading the Torah during Purim celebrations.

unity that an author gives to a piece of writing. Not only that, but the Bible does not even have a single editor or compiler. Someone drew together and edited the first five books, the 'Pentateuch'. Someone gathered together the collection of liturgical poetry that we call 'The Psalms'. Someone else edited the 'Wisdom' books – Proverbs, Ecclesiastes and the rest. Beyond that, at some point a decision was made that certain books and collections would be the Hebrew Scriptures, the sacred writings that would define both a nation (Israel) and a religion (Judaism).

When we turn to the New Testament, we face the same questions. We have one advantage here, because several of the authors identify themselves, either directly or by inference. Nevertheless, the decision had to be made – and was, after several centuries of argument and debate – as to which writings were, or were not, qualified to be regarded as the Christian Scriptures, the writings that would define a new community (the church) and a new religion (Christianity). The decision was made by the church and, broadly speaking, has been accepted by Christians of every tradition ever since.

The Bible as we now have it has two main sections, the Hebrew Scriptures (the 'Bible' Jesus knew, which we call the 'Old Testament') and the Christian Scriptures, the 'New Testament'.

The Hebrew Scriptures

Although the order of the books is different, the Hebrew Scriptures are virtually identical with the 'Old Testament'. They had developed into their current form by the second century BC, and are divided into three sections – the Law, the Prophets and the Writings. The oldest section, the Law (or the 'Pentateuch' – the first five books of the Bible) was complete in its present form and accepted as having divine authority certainly by the time of Ezra and Nehemiah (fifth century BC).

Because of the way the books are divided, there are only thirty-six books in the Hebrew Scriptures, compared to the thirty-nine in the Christian Old Testament, even though the material is identical. The Prophets are placed in the Hebrew Bible after Kings (which is one, not two books) and before Psalms and the other Wisdom books, such as Psalms, Job, Ruth and Ecclesiastes. Chronicles (again one book, not two) is the last book of the Hebrew Scriptures.

The Christian Scriptures

The New Testament starts with the four 'Gospels', telling through different perspectives the story of the life, teaching, death and resurrection of Jesus. They are followed by the 'Acts of the Apostles', which is an account of the early years of the church. The 'Epistles' (letters) of Paul, Peter, James and John follow, showing how the message of the gospel was worked out in the early days of the church. The New Testament ends with the book of Revelation, with its warnings, prophecies and promises about the future. The 'canon' (the list of recognized books) was finalized early in the fifth century AD, but the list of recognized books has not changed much since the end of the second century.

So the Bible is a kind of anthology or symposium of books by many different authors, brought together at different times and in different places by a variety of editors or compilers, most of them completely unknown to us. Yet I have claimed that it has a 'plot', or 'tells a story'; in fact, that there is some sense of unity or purpose running through it. We move here into the realm of faith, I suppose, but I think that even the sceptical or questioning reader will sense that the whole is greater than the sum of the parts. The Bible is not, and doesn't read like, a random selection of writings. That's why it helps, even on a first approach to it, to have in mind the 'plot' or story that runs through it.

The Story of a Nation

For instance, why should it contain so much about the history and ideas of one small Middle Eastern nation, Israel? This story takes up two-thirds of the Bible, at least. One might feel that something important or significant must have been happening somewhere else – and indeed it was. The Bible, as I have said, is essentially an account of humanity's search for God, and God's ways with humanity. Was he all through those ages of prehistory and history saying and doing nothing to and for the peoples of the other nations of the world? It would of course be strange if he wasn't, and there are hints in various stories in the Hebrew Scriptures of his dealings with other races. But what we are offered here is the story of a single thread of divine purpose, slowly making its way through the history of one people, painfully teaching and leading them, until from that people and their history came the person who would show not only that people but the whole world the purpose of the God who was their Creator.

You don't have to believe it to agree that that is a noble and vast concept. It starts from the premise that the God who made the human race is a God of revelation: he actually wants us to know him and his purposes. He is not a silent God, but a God who 'speaks'. The pages of these strange and varied books, through many different modes and media, try to record the story of that revelation, to capture in its stories, poetry, chronicles and visions the words and actions of the God who wants us to know him and his purposes. That is why Christians down the ages *have* identified a single author or editor – no less than the Holy Spirit of God.

2

The Bible: History?

You don't need to get far into the
Bible – the first three chapters will
do – to discover that it sets itself in
history. Unlike some of the other
great religious books of the world,
like the Bhagavad Gita, for
instance, it is not simply a
collection of stories, dialogue and
wise sayings largely detached from
historical points of reference. The
Bible sets itself in history, pretty
well right from the first chapters. This poses an immediate problem
for the modern reader.

If this is a book written within human history – indeed, if it claims
to be part of that history – does that mean that we should judge the
Bible by normal historical criteria. Is it true? Did it really happen like
that? Are its accounts of 'events' reliable at the factual level? Or is it a
different 'take' on history, concerned with some kind of truth within
history that is greater or deeper than the mere 'facts'?

Truth Greater Than 'Facts'

The dilemma can be illustrated in this way. In the first few chapters
of the Bible, we launch straight into an account of the creation, in
some detail with regard to order and origins, only to find that the
second chapter offers us another account, this time focused on the
creation of the human race, male and female. Chapter 3 offers us
what seems to be another kind of 'history': the wicked serpent-
tempter in the Garden of Eden, and the banishment of the Man and

the Woman, by now named Adam and Eve, from their earthly paradise for eating the forbidden fruit. Chapter 4 records the first crime: two of Adam's sons falling out and Cain murdering Abel. Chapter 5 offers an astonishing gallery of geriatrics, a genealogy of early human beings who apparently lived to quite extraordinary ages, led by the fabled Methuselah, who, it is recorded, lived to be 969. In chapter 6 we begin the account of the flood and of Noah's survival of it by building the ark.

By now the average reader new to the Bible will be wondering what's going on. Is this myth, fable, legend or, as some of it certainly seems to purport to be, an attempt at historical narrative, a kind of chronicle of humankind's early days on earth? Even accepting, as we surely must, that the Bible

The Creation of Adam by Michelangelo Buonarroti (1475–1564). The great artist tried to capture in this wonderful fresco the moment when God gave life to Adam. The story of creation is beyond factual reporting (or even artistic illustration), but the picture shows how human imagination can explore the powerful imagery of the biblical story.

includes widely diverse literary modes, this seems to be pushing a few frontiers to their limits.

The Words and Works of God

Most people, indeed most Christians, would have no problem in reading the opening chapter of Genesis as something other than straight historical and scientific reportage. At the same time, it does appear to claim enormous authority for itself. These are the words and works of God, no less. This is not offered as merely a 'point of view', nor even just 'one way of seeing it'. It's all very well to claim, as many Christians do, that this is a religious rather than a historical or scientific treatise, but they still seem to attach to it an authority and authenticity that one would not normally ascribe to fantasy literature, however profound, ingenious or persuasive. The modern mind constantly nags away: but is it *true*?

THE FLOOD

Many ancient cultures have preserved a story about a great flood which only a few people survived. The biblical story probably echoes the same memory, passed on through a long tradition of oral repetition, probably in story form, but here seen as a distinct and specific act of God. Some terrible moral corruption had polluted the human race – Genesis 6:1–3 hints that it may have involved inter-marriage between humans and other humanoid species – and the Flood is seen as a massive cleansing operation. Noah and his family represent the 'godly remnant', a familiar theme of the Hebrew Scriptures. His obedience brought about his salvation and that of his family, and also (in the best-known aspect of the story) that of the animal and bird kingdom. When the Flood had abated, God promised that he would never again judge the world in this devastating way, but that the seasons would continue uninterrupted to the end of time (Genesis 8:21, 22).

To answer that satisfactorily, one has to grapple with the whole idea of 'truth'. Does truth lie in 'facts'? Or in my own experience of life? Or in the interpretation of life by wise and inspiring leaders and teachers? Or in some accumulated wisdom handed on through the long ages of human existence? Is it the by-product of cool, scientific 'evidence', backed up by careful research and ruthless analysis of its results? Or none of these?

What is Truth?

In thirty years as a working journalist I learned a healthy scepticism for 'facts', and to be doubly sceptical of journalists or broadcasters who claimed to be offering me 'the facts' about almost anything. Truth is deeper, more elusive, than that, and as a matter of faith I would now say that truth, in the ultimate sense,

The Entry of the Animals into Noah's Ark by Jan Brueghel the Elder (1568–1625).

has to be God-given. With all of that in mind, it might be rewarding to look again at that opening chapter of the Bible. To start with, there could not possibly be any human observer of the creation of the universe, so that the only source of such knowledge would be the Creator. Assuming that the Creator wished to provide the human race with a comprehensive factual account of the origins of the universe, it is hard to imagine in what form it could have been couched in order to be equally intelligible to people in the pre-scientific age and those of more recent times.

What we have, in fact, in these opening chapters of Genesis, is an astonishingly powerful piece of writing which can be and is appreciated by modern-day physicists and biologists, and yet spoke equally intensely to the people of the pre-scientific era in which the story was first recorded. What the opening chapter offers is a vivid narrative, written as poetry, not prose (notice the recurring chorus, 'There was evening and there was morning, the third day,' and so on) which lays the platform for the fundamental argument of the whole Bible: this world is a creation, not an accident, and human beings are creatures within it. In this way, a very profound case is set out in language that is intelligible to people of every age, speaking with the same power and authority to today's astrophysicist as it would have done to our distant ancestors in their tents.

Centuries of Retelling

We may well feel that what follows in these early chapters of the Bible, dealing with what might be called 'prehistory', is of a similar genre. Some of it is in poetic language, but most is in the language either of the storyteller (which we discuss in chapter 3) or of the chronicler. By the time these ancient stories were first written down, some time in the first millennium before Christ, they had been shaped and polished and adapted by centuries of retelling. As we shall see later, stories are not untruths, necessarily, but truth told in a different way, and most Christians today would have little difficulty in seeing a divine providence at work in the way these narratives were handed down, preserving for us precious insights into the nature of the creation in which we live and the race to which we belong. Undoubtedly there are substantial historical memories here; of ancestors of great renown, of a mighty flood from which few were saved, and of the gradual dispersal of the fledgling human race from its original location in the Middle

East (or wherever) to distant lands, where language changed beyond recognition. All of this we can find in the first eleven chapters of Genesis, though the richness of the truths they convey will be largely lost on those who demand that they should be factual records, and argue over who was Cain's wife or the identity of the Nephilim (Genesis 6:4).

That leaves us with the question: how should we read the Bible's 'history'? If it is more than 'facts', does it matter if it's less than them? Is its authenticity compromised if a chronicler gets the numbers wrong about those engaged in a battle, or spells the name of a monarch differently from other ancient records? Closer to home, as it were, does it matter that Luke, in his Gospel, seems to have made a trivial mistake over the dates when Quirinius was governor of Syria, or that the Gospels seem to give contradictory accounts of the death of the miserable traitor, Judas?

Did Jonah Swallow the Whale?

For some Christians it certainly does matter. I remember being told, in my early days of instruction in the faith, that if one were to doubt the claim that Balaam's ass spoke (Numbers 22:28), how could one be sure that the Bible was telling the truth about the resurrection of Jesus? The speaker boasted that if the Bible said that Jonah swallowed the whale, instead of *vice versa*, he would believe it. I thought then, and I think now, that God would not ask human beings to whom he has given intelligence and reason to act so grotesquely in defiance of them.

Is it, then, more a matter of what I can 'swallow' than of what Jonah or the whale could? That would turn the reading of the Bible into an exercise in entirely personal interpretation: the Bible means what I am prepared to take it to mean. At once it is emasculated, shorn of any vestige of authority or even objective value. Like some character in Lewis Carroll's *Alice in Wonderland*, I simply declare that it means what I want it to mean.

That would surely be far too subjective a position to adopt. It reduces the Bible to one simple test: can I bring myself to believe this, or not? And if I can't, then the Bible is useless to me and valueless as a source of truth. On that criterion, we should have to abandon any idea that is at present beyond our comprehension. For instance, how do I 'swallow' the notion of the existence of the

Battle scene from a relief in the Palace of King Sennacherib at Nineveh. Assyrian troops are depicted besieging the Judean city of Lachish in the year 701 BC, an event recorded in 2 Kings 18:13.

THE BIBLE AND ARCHAEOLOGICAL DISCOVERIES

There have been many instances in the last century of archaeological discoveries that have confirmed the accuracy of the biblical record, even where for a long while scholars had cast doubts on it. They include discoveries of inscriptions and artefacts as well as bits of manuscript. For instance, in 1961 an inscription was found at Caesarea bearing the name of Pontius Pilate, the first such evidence to be established for the Roman prefect who sentenced Jesus to death. However, it is notoriously difficult to find hard evidence for events that took place more than two thousand years ago, let alone in patriarchal days perhaps two thousand years before that.

The guiding principle in all historical analysis is source – who wrote the account, and why? Time and again the evidence is that much of the Bible (except those parts that are poetry, allegory or vision) is a book set firmly in human history, written by real people (some identified, some not) about real events and experiences, either as they themselves experienced them or as they were handed down to them through traditional narratives.

---

universe itself, or of time and space, of self-consciousness, of relativity or gravity or anything else that I accept on trust but cannot fully comprehend for myself? If all truth can be tested solely by what I can accept at this moment, or at my present level of understanding, then relatively little would go into the portfolio. Certainly to approach the Bible with that attitude will close our minds to all manner of wonderful insights and glimpses of truth. We may not come with a confident, committed faith, but we need to come with open minds and imaginations ready to engage with unfamiliar concepts.

In making a judgment about the historicity of biblical texts, there are surely some principles to shape our approach. I would like to suggest four.

What Kind of a Text is This?

First of all, there is the principle of literary analysis: asking, 'What kind of a text is this?' If it is poetry, then different criteria of truth apply. If it is allegory, or myth, or apocalyptic literature – which has some of the marks of modern fantasy writing – then again we approach it in a different way from historical reportage. As we shall see, this process is absolutely vital in reading the Bible, if only because it encompasses so many different literary genres, often in the same book, or even part of a book.

Where Does it Come From?

Secondly, what is its provenance (as they say in antique showrooms)? What is its own history and background? Does it come from prehistory, probably first told and retold around village campfires for centuries before being committed to writing? Or does it come from a particular pressure group or school of thought within a culture? Is it didactic – setting out to teach a truth or convince a doubter? Does it weave stories into what seems to be an otherwise historical framework, either to make a point or to invite the reader to see the question in a new and different way?

To take concrete examples, there is a world of difference between the provenance of the Gospels, written, for the most part, within forty or fifty years of the events they relate, and the book of Genesis or the book of Exodus, where the events they describe (or the story they tell) are far removed in time from their recording in writing, much less their incorporation into the Hebrew and then the Christian Scriptures.

Where Does it 'Fit' in the Whole Story?

The third principle to be applied is probably the most important. Where does this text find its place in the whole story of the relationship between God and the human race? The Gospels, though posing a set of questions of their own, are easy to place. So, in its own way, is Genesis, which traces origins: the origins of the universe, of life and of people. It also bravely tackles the problem of the relationship between belief in God and practical hope for our planet and its inhabitants. Equally bravely, it offers an 'explanation' of the presence of evil in a universe created by a good God, and deemed by him to be 'very good' (Genesis 1:31).

Going back to the 'plot' I proposed in the opening chapter, where does each part fit into the whole? Seeing a piece of writing in its whole context is often the vital clue to understanding it properly – and that's as true of an article in today's newspaper as it is of the story of Adam and Eve.

The Real World

The fourth principle is a simple but important one: that the Bible is set in the context of human history. It puts itself into real time and real space. It never sees itself as utterly detached from the world we live in and the people we are, even when, as in Revelation, it soars through unimaginable realms of visionary experience. The man who has those visions is on the island of Patmos (a place) on a Sunday (at a time), and his name is John. Make what we will of the visions, this is a human experience, within the parameters of time and space. These writings are for us, where we are, and when we are. They are not make-believe, and they are not intended for gods or angels but for human eyes, minds and hearts.

I began this chapter by asking whether the Bible was concerned with some different 'take' on history, concerned with a kind of truth within history that is greater or deeper than the mere 'facts'. I hope that I have at least made a case for reading it in that way, not as though all of it is simple fiction, the product of a fertile, albeit spiritually aware, human imagination, but looking all the while for the truth it is seeking to convey. We may find it in the Bible's poetry, or its stories and allegories, or in its wise words and proverbs. We may find it in the chronicles of an ancient people's search for the living God, and of God's search for them. We may find it more clearly than elsewhere in the most intentionally 'factual' section of the Christian Bible, the Gospels, where we meet the astounding figure of Jesus of Nazareth. It is everywhere to be found, but the reader has to do the looking. That is the challenge of the Bible to its would-be reader.

3
The Bible as Story Book

'You're telling stories' means, in everyday English, 'You're making it up' – or, more bluntly, it's all a pack of lies. That's why it's hard to talk of the Bible as a 'story book'. People immediately assume that you mean that it's all just fiction, a collection of tales which over the centuries has somehow developed a mystical or spiritual authority.

In fact, in human experience stories have been the staple fare of history. Hannibal crossing the Alps, George Washington and the cherry tree, Robin Hood in Sherwood Forest, and Joan of Arc and her divine mission – these are stories (partly true, partly embellished in the retelling) which most people have heard and enjoyed, but we also know that behind them are real people and some genuine history. The stories were told to relate that history to human experience, to 'humanize' it, I suppose.

Modern Stories

In modern times stories have been used in the same way: Khrushchev standing astride a Soviet tank on the streets of Moscow; a Chinese student defying tanks in Tiannamen Square in Beijing; the little boats of Dunkirk; the demolition of the infamous Berlin Wall; the hijacked planes hitting New York's Twin Towers; and the tottering statue of Saddam Hussein in Baghdad. What are these but vivid stories which capture for us great moments of history? In many cases the stories will be remembered when the events that gave them their context are recorded only in the dusty archives of museums.

Stories give life to events and ideas. It is in that sense that the Bible is a storybook. It doesn't present its readers, for the most part, with propositions and argument, but with stories and people.

This was precisely the approach of Jesus, who presented some of his most subtle teaching in the stories which we call 'parables' – 'it's as if...' sayings. Even when the Bible is recounting events that it wishes us to understand as historical, they are usually told with the art of the storyteller rather than the technique of the historian.

A good story requires skill and imagination from its teller, but it also needs imagination and perception from its hearer. That seems to be the meaning of the rather strange saying of Jesus, which closes many of his parables: 'He who has ears to hear, let him hear.' It's as though he were saying, 'That's my story. Now make it yours.' He invited his hearers (and therefore his readers today) to use their God-given gifts of imagination and faith to interpret and apply his deceptively simple and homely stories. A sower with his seed, a merchant buying pearls, a fisherman with his net, a dodgy steward and his accounts – listen to these stories about them, says Jesus, and then decide what they say to you about yourself.

The Bible's 'Stories'

In this chapter I want to look at a few of the Bible's stories and to invite you to think of them in that way, as *stories*, even if your first instinct is to treat them with reverence as sacred teachings, or even perhaps with scorn as a load of nonsense. Sometimes you can have too much reverence. Sometimes our presuppositions become baggage, which obscures the truth a simple tale is offering to us. And sometimes we are too quick to be scornful, thinking, in that cynical manner which marks our generation, that we know better, that simple tales from long ago can teach nothing to a scientific age like ours.

As we turn to consider these stories, it's important to try to think of them as spoken, rather than written. Try to hear them as though you were sitting around the fire in the middle of an encampment, or at the feet of a gifted storyteller in a dusty Middle Eastern street. Remove from your mind, if you can, the solemn binding and gilt edging of the traditional Bible, and *listen to the story*.

The Garden of Delights

Let's start at the beginning, with the Garden of Eden. The story is narrated in Genesis chapters 2 and 3. Although the first chapter of this book recorded the creation of human beings made 'in the image of God – male and female', we now move from the language of poetry and theology to the language of story.

We start with a moment of high drama. God scoops a handful of dust from the ground he has created and from it he forms a man. Then he 'breathes into his nostrils the breath of life'. Having put the first character of the story in place, he now creates the scene. He plants a garden 'eastward in Eden', and puts the man in it. In the garden many delights were on offer: trees 'pleasant to the sight and good for food', a river to water the soil, and nearby supplies of gold, bdellium and the onyx stone. God also gave the man pleasant work to do, tilling and cultivating the garden and enjoying its delights. He even provided him with animals and birds for company, and cattle for milk and cream.

However, he still lacked one delight: human company. God said, 'It is not good that the man should be alone.' So woman was created, shaped from the man's rib, 'bone of my bones and flesh of my flesh', as the man said delightedly. He clung to his wife and they became, in the language of the Bible, 'one flesh'.

Now, surely, all would be well in the Garden of Delights? What more could the first two human beings want? Sun, sensuous delights, sumptuous food, riches untold, and now delightful, innocent sex. Yet there was a question that clearly perplexed them. Why had they been forbidden by God to eat the fruit of the tree that was in the middle of the garden? Why this arbitrary rule? Thus early in the Bible's story we are coming face to face with human nature as we all know it: curious, argumentative, independent, assertive. The wretched tree in the middle of Eden bugged them, and as the story progresses that thought becomes fuel for a very unpleasant tempter to work on.

Temptation – and Fall

This tempter is usually called the serpent, though the word used could equally well mean any kind of animal. Like a character in one of Aesop's fables, it began by planting doubts in the woman's mind. Sidling up to her, it asked, 'Did God really say that you mustn't eat of that particular tree? Surely not! What harm could that do? Actually, God knows that if you were to eat it you would become like him, "knowing good and evil".' The woman looked at the fruit on the

The story of the 'serpent' who tempted Eve has led to many myths and misunderstandings about snakes. To start with, the creature that uttered the tempting words (even on the most literal reading) was simply 'one of the animals that the Lord God had made' (Genesis 3:1) rather than a snake as we know it. However, the curse on him sounds like the transformation of an animal with legs to one that slides along on its belly (Genesis 3:14) – though the second part of the curse ('dust you shall eat all the days of your life'), although widely believed until modern times, is quite untrue – snakes eat quite a varied diet!

The seer of Revelation has a vision of an 'ancient serpent' being finally overthrown by Michael and his angels. He identifies him as the one who is called 'the devil and Satan, the deceiver of the whole world' (Revelation 12:9). So it is probably best simply to think of this creature as the personification of all opposition to the will of God, which is more or less what the name 'Satan' (the Hebrew word for 'adversary') means.

Adam and Eve by Lucas Cranach the Elder (1472–1553).

tree, now even more attractive: good for food, 'a delight to the eyes' and – she now hears – a possible source of divine wisdom. There was no stopping her. She took the fruit, ate it, and gave some to the man to eat as well. Nothing too alarming happened, but for the first time in their lives they noticed that they were naked, and so made loin cloths of fig leaves to cover their private parts.

In the cool of the evening God made an appearance in the garden. The man and the woman hid themselves in the bushes, but God called for them and the man ventured a response. 'I was frightened when I heard your voice, because I was naked, so I hid.' God's reply is interesting. 'Who told you that you were naked?' – as though here was the clue to their confusion and guilt, the loss of innocence. The man searched for a scapegoat. 'The woman you gave me, she gave me fruit from the tree, and I ate.' It was a clever move, attempting to put the blame not only on the woman but, by inference, on God himself – 'the woman *you gave me*'.

God's attention now turned to the woman. 'What have you done?' But she also found herself a scapegoat. 'The serpent tricked me, and I ate.' When it came to the serpent's turn, there were no scapegoats left – we might say, it hadn't a leg to stand on.

All that remained for each miscreant was for the punishments to be spelt out. From now on the serpent would be cursed among all animals, travelling on his belly and eating only the dust of the ground. There would be constant enmity between his offspring and the woman's; the former would strike at the latters' heels, the latter would strike at the formers' heads.

The punishments for the disobedient woman and her husband similarly mirror subsequent experience. The woman would have pain in childbirth and be under the domination of her husband. For his part, work would from now on be a sore trial: 'By the sweat of your face you shall eat bread until you return to the ground from which you were taken.' Having laid these penalties on them, God clothed the man and woman in garments made of skins – more permanent than fig leaves? – and ordered them out of the garden, away from the place of delight to the unknown lands of exploitation and gruelling labour.

Magical Mystery?

That's the story, and the reader may well feel that J. K. Rowling could have done it just as well – indeed, that it falls into that genre of magical mystery with a touch of horror that people have always enjoyed in the telling. This story, however, is not Rowling, or Hans Christian Andersen, but part of the Bible, the sacred Scriptures that have helped to mould our civilization. Does anything distinguish it from them, pull us up sharp and say, 'That's speaking to me at a different level altogether'?

Maybe not, at first acquaintance. But a closer reading may reveal greater treasures. In Jewish and Christian thinking, this story is fundamental, which is presumably why it stands where it does in the Bible. It offers an answer to the question that every thoughtful human being will ask sooner or later: Where did evil come from? What's its origin? It doesn't tackle it philosophically or sociologically, and it doesn't look for the explanation in our genes or even our nurture, yet it does, in the form of a story that a child could follow, set out an approach to the problem of evil that undergirds the rest of the biblical understanding of it.

The Risks of Choice

The story shows us a man and a woman in a world without evil, a world of total innocence. Yet there are unanswered questions for them. If God has made them 'in his

Apollo XI astronaut Neil Armstrong leaves a footprint on the surface of the Moon at Tranquility Base, 20 July, 1969.

ONE GIANT STEP...?

Neil Armstrong, the American astronaut who in July 1969 became the first man to set foot on the Moon, described it as a 'giant step for mankind'. That expedition, in which Buzz Aldrin also walked on the Moon, was simply one more example of the human desire to explore our environment, even if it involves (as the Apollo XI mission did) enormous risks. In fact, human curiosity knows no bounds and seems blind to potential dangers.

This suggests that the Genesis story of Adam and Eve in the Garden of Eden is entirely consistent with what we know about human nature. The forbidden fruit was there. Why not eat it? A similar reason is given for climbing Everest – 'because it's there!' Of course there was a huge element of risk for Adam and Eve – their Creator had forbidden it. But the risk was taken and the choice was made.

own image', then surely, like God, they must be able to make choices, and make them about more profound things than which fruit to have for breakfast or whether to make love at lunch time or in the cool of the evening. And the garden – the very place where God has set them – offers those weightier choices. Should the woman try the fruit from the forbidden tree? If she did, would the man follow her? Everything we know from our own 'internal' human experience tells us that they would. Choices inevitably involve risk, and the human race has always taken risks. If we hadn't, we should still be cowering in caves hiding from wild beasts and eating nothing but berries and fruit.

Our sense of risk, however, is more profound than that. We are insatiably curious, so that the question 'Why?' nags away at us like an aching tooth. We want to know, even if knowing puts security at risk. Being persons, possessing self-conscious personalities, we share God's own delight in creating, exploring, yes, taking risks (for surely the creation of human beings was the greatest risk there could be). Without it, God would simply have peopled his world with robots programmed to do his will, or angels whose sole delight it was to do it. Instead, he took the daring option of creating beings 'in his own image', possessing a God-given gift of moral autonomy: the right to choose whether or not they wished to serve him, whether or not they would live by his will, whether or not they would love or hate him. As I have said, that seems a risk of truly cosmic significance.

So what is the role of the 'serpent', the tempter? It (or he) is identified later in the Bible as 'Satan', literally, 'the adversary'. He (or it) is, in other words, the embodiment or personification of that which is 'against' God – the Leader of the Opposition, we might say. In terms of this story, for instance, he is surely putting into words what the woman, and probably the man, was already thinking: what a silly, arbitrary rule – as though God doesn't trust us to use the fruit of the forbidden tree wisely and in an adult way! It must be more significant than that, to justify so arbitrary a ban – so what is it? Some hidden wisdom or knowledge? Some deep, untapped pleasure known only to God? As soon as human beings start asking the questions, the risk becomes all but irresistible.

The End of Innocence
So the fruit was eaten, and everything changes. Innocence flees. Guilt makes its entrance. And so does judgment, the judgment of

God. The freedom they have seized carries inbuilt penalties, which they and their descendants must now learn to live with.

The two examples given are so relevant to human experience that they hardly need spelling out. Women would be exploited and dominated by the physically stronger sex, the males, and childbirth would involve anxiety and pain. For men work, which in God's creation could have been a creative joy, would turn out to be hard, wearisome, unproductive and unrewarding. In my own pastoral experience I would say that the majority of women presenting a deep problem in their lives would want to talk about a man (or men); and most men wishing to discuss what troubles them would start with work. Whoever wrote this story knew the human experience well, and if it is, as Christians believe, in some mysterious way inspired by God, then that is, I suppose, no more than we would expect.

That element of spiritual insight can be found not only in the matter of the 'curses' laid on the man and the woman, but throughout the whole story. Two approaches seem to me particularly unhelpful in reading it. One is to set out to defend every detail as literal, historical fact, which reduces it to a highly suspect piece of reportage and robs it of its divine 'mystery'. The other is to treat it as something of a joke – an approach often taken in children's books of Bible stories.

In fact, it is a tragedy, and if it evokes tears they should be of sorrow rather than mirth. Here is our story, the universal experience of our race, laid out before us in all its monumental folly. After all, the sin of the man and the woman – not named as 'Adam' and 'Eve' until they are expelled from the garden – is rooted in the most fundamental failing of our race, its conviction that we know better than our Creator. The 'forbidden apple' wasn't sex, but pride. The woman was led astray by a simple question: '*Did* God say...?' Allow the question to take root and it will soon take not roots but wings. It is very, very hard for us to accept that the Creator knows best what is for our good, but doubting it is the worm in the apple, the insidious thought that will eventually lead us to follow our own inclination, whatever we may know or suppose to be the will of God. Even as I struggle to put this into words, I can see how the story does the task so much better!

Loaves and Fish

We move from a story set in prehistory to one which we can place and date, indeed one which beyond reasonable doubt describes an event which actually happened. It is told four times in the New Testament, once in each of the Gospels, and each time in the form of a story, and it is as a story that I want us to read it.

The event is easily described, though the different Gospel writers each add little details of their own. A crowd had followed Jesus as he preached, eventually congregating in large numbers in a deserted rural spot far from shops or homes. The disciples of Jesus point out to him that evening is fast approaching and that the people are hungry. They can't be sent off to find their way home without some food inside them. Jesus tells them to feed the crowd themselves – a hopeless task, they point out, with such a vast crowd and no available supplies. The Gospels claim that five thousand people were present in the crowd. While we may respectfully doubt the precise numerical accuracy of that figure (no calculators were available), it is clear that a very large number needed to be fed. One Gospel mentions a boy who offered his own supper of five bread rolls and two small fish. The others simply relate the bafflement of the disciples at the

This beautiful fifth-century mosaic of the loaves and fishes is to be found in a church at Tabgha by the Sea of Galilee, which marks the traditional site of the miracle of 'The Feeding of the Five Thousand'.

enormity of the challenge. Two hundred days' wages would not buy enough bread for a crowd of that size, they told Jesus.

In the event, Jesus takes what they have – five small loaves and two fish. He gives thanks for them, breaks them and gives them to the disciples to distribute to the people. When that is done, each Gospel notes in identical words, 'they all ate and were satisfied'. The disciples are then sent to gather up the crumbs and fragments left over, and collect twelve small baskets full – more food than they had started with.

Raising Doubts

'The Feeding of the Five Thousand' is a well-known miracle story from the New Testament, but it raises many doubts in modern minds. How did the miracle occur? Was the bread and fish supernaturally multiplied as Jesus blessed it? Or was it that, as the disciples broke and shared it out, the bread and fish simply replenished itself? Or was it all an illusion on a mass scale, brought on by hunger under the fierce sun? Or was it, as has been memorably suggested, simply an exercise in corporate sandwich sharing: the boy's supper was offered to Jesus for distribution and everyone else was shamed into doing the same?

The last two of these 'explanations' will not work, it seems to me. If this was a mass delusion, then it truly was on the grand scale! As for the sandwich suggestion, one can only assume that as this is the only miracle of Jesus recorded in all four Gospels, each writer thought it of such importance that it demanded inclusion. Would an exercise in shared picnics have been so momentous that all four felt it simply *must* be included in their Gospel?

Surely a better explanation is that something so extraordinary, so remarkable and so significant occurred in this miracle that a life of Jesus without it would be incomplete?

Not 'How' but 'Why'?

It's a reasonable deduction, then, that in some way which the writers can't, and don't even try to explain, a crowd in the country were fed at the end of a long day in the sun. Of course, they *do* offer an explanation, but not of the 'how?' variety. They are more interested in something else: *why?* Why did Jesus take fish and bread, bless it, break it, give it to his disciples and ask them to share it with the people? And why does each writer – despite other small variations and additions to the narrative – end with precisely the same words: 'All ate and were satisfied'? And why the odd detail of the crumbs collected in the baskets?

One Gospel, John's, points to some answers to those questions. He follows the story with an extended dialogue between Jesus and members of the crowd and his own followers. In the course of this he explicitly links what he has just done to what Moses did in the wilderness during the forty-year journey of the Israelites from Egypt to their promised land. Moses fed the people with 'manna', the strange 'bread from heaven' which nourished them on their pilgrimage. Though, as Jesus points out, it wasn't Moses who provided the manna, but God. He fed their forefathers with this 'heavenly' food, but eventually, of course, they all died. Now Jesus was feeding God's 'new' Israel, his disciples, with 'heavenly' food – and he would do more than that. If they believed in him, they would have eternal life, because he, Jesus, is the 'bread of life'.

The Breaking of Bread

All of that, of course, is John's commentary on the miracle of the feeding of the five thousand; the 'theological' explanation of it, as we might say. But even without John's help, the early Christians in the churches of the first and second centuries would probably have made their own connections, because what Jesus did on the hillside was described in the Gospels in words which also described precisely what they saw each week as they gathered for the 'breaking of bread', Holy Communion. Notice the exact language, again the same in each Gospel: Jesus took the bread, blessed it, broke it, gave it to the disciples and told them to distribute it to the people. And when they had, everyone was 'filled', satisfied. They might, like us, have struggled with the mechanics of the miracle, but the meaning of the story would have been as clear as daylight. Jesus feeds us. He takes ordinary bread, as their presbyter/elder did each week, blesses and breaks it, and when his assistants, the deacons, bring it to us, we are satisfied. More than that, his generosity is such that there is plenty left over for others! On the journey of faith, none need go unfed.

So, in a story of exceptional power and relevance, based (as I have argued) on an event witnessed by many people, the Gospel writers convey a message of deep significance. We might argue about the 'facts', but we can't argue about the story. It speaks to anyone who hears it or reads it. All of us know what hunger is, it says. Well, in Jesus all our hungers can be satisfied.

Walking on the Water

I would like to look at one more story of a miracle from the New Testament, again one that is well known, if only for the detail that in it Jesus is said to 'walk on water'. Two of the Gospels (Matthew and Mark) record this miracle, along with another rather similar one of a storm on the lake when Jesus was with his disciples in a boat. Galilee was a province situated around the lake of that name, and one of its main industries was fishing. In fact, four of Jesus' disciples were fishermen by trade. Stories about the lake, fishing and boats are to be expected in Gospels that are based on events largely in that territory.

This story, however, is rather different. The bare facts of the narrative, substantially the same in both Gospels, are these. Jesus sent his disciples off in a boat one evening to cross the lake while he remained on a hillside alone, praying. As the evening wore on a strong wind arose – not an unfamiliar phenomenon on Galilee with its narrow valleys at the north and south ends. It was against the disciples as they rowed their boat, and was so powerful that they could make no progress, but merely kept head on into it to avoid capsizing. In the early hours of the morning, Jesus became aware of their plight and – say the Gospels – 'came walking towards them on the water'. When they saw this they were terrified, saying, 'It's a ghost!' Jesus spoke to them and said, 'Take heart. It is I; don't be afraid.'

Peter and the Waves

Matthew adds a fascinating subplot at this point. Peter, always one for a challenge, questioned the figure walking on the waves. 'If it *is* you, Lord, command me to come to you on the water.' Jesus said, 'Come,' and Peter got out of the boat and started walking on the water towards him. But 'when he noticed the strong wind' he became frightened, and began to sink. He shouted to Jesus to help him, and Jesus reached out a hand and caught him, asking why he had 'doubted'. As they climbed into the boat both Gospels record that the wind ceased, and 'those in the boat worshipped him, saying, "Truly you are the Son of God."'

How – or Why?

That is the story as given to us, dramatic enough even for the urban landlubber, and spellbinding, one would assume, for a group of men all but one of whom had grown up around the lake and learned to respect its moods and its occasional ferocity. The modern reader or listener, however, will probably have a different reaction. Once again, I suspect it is a kind of polite incredulity. We will be asking how it happened; how Jesus could defy the laws of physics and walk across the surface of the water. I don't suppose that question bothered the first hearers one jot. They would have been asking an equally searching – and rather more important – question: 'Why tell me this story? What does it mean?'

It's that reaction which the Gospel writers are concerned with. For them, this was like an acted parable, its message vivid and relevant. One or two background facts are perhaps important if we are to read or hear it with first-century eyes and ears. In the first place, the Jews of those days hated the sea. For them it held many nameless terrors. In fact, one of the visions of heaven in the book of Revelation might surprise people today: there will be 'no more sea'! That ugly menacing cauldron of mystery would be gone for ever; the untameable would be tamed.

The Nameless Terrors of Life

So the sea (the lake, in this case) came to represent the nameless terrors of life, the events and situations that create fear and deep anxiety. Out on the lake in the darkness of the small hours, making no headway, their little flat-bottomed boat tossed by wind and waves, the disciples of Jesus were terrified. There is the picture of every nameless fear of the human heart; irrational, perhaps, but destructive of peace and security. The sea seemed to have them in its power, until, miracle of miracles, Jesus came to them 'walking across the water'. He came to them across the very subject of their terror, showed that it held no terror for him; indeed, that he was its lord and master.

Then there were the words that Jesus spoke. 'Do not be afraid; it is I.' Literally, the last phrase is 'I am' – *ego eimi*. For them, the very name of God, Yahweh, I AM, sounded from his lips. How could they fear? Their God, no less, was coming to them in their plight. We could say (to put it in religious language) that their Saviour was here. The storm ceased; and we may ask *which* storm – the one that disturbed the waves, or the one that disturbed their hearts? Or, of course, both?

The Peter story is interesting because Mark *doesn't* include it, although it is generally reckoned (on good internal evidence) that

THE SEA OF GALILEE

Galilee is a lake in north-east Israel which in biblical times gave its name to the surrounding region. It is fed by water from the mountains to the north, including Mount Hermon, and the River Jordan runs from its southern tip. The lake is 14 miles (23 km) long and about 5 miles (8 km) wide. Lying below sea level and fed by warm mineral springs, it has always been a plentiful source of fish, notably the unique 'Peter's fish'.

With natural gaps at both the north and south ends, it is peculiarly vulnerable to sudden storms caused by the 'wind-tunnel' effect. The boats used in biblical times were flat-bottomed wooden vessels – one was recently excavated from the bed of the lake and restored. They were not well designed to cope with high winds or waves, though highly suited for their primary purpose of fishing using spread nets.

Peter was a source for his material. That could mean that Peter didn't want to appear to boast (after all, he at least tried, while the others cowered in the boat), or that he was slightly ashamed of his actions, first doubting whether the figure really was Jesus, and then losing faith when faced with the wind and waves.

Asleep in the Stern

There is, of course, another 'storm on Lake Galilee' story in the Gospels, one in which Jesus is already in the boat with the disciples, but is so untroubled by the storm that he is asleep in the stern. In that story, Jesus is *with* his followers in their distress and anxiety, whereas in the walking-on-the-water episode he is not there, but praying for them from a distance – a situation that will become the norm after his return to his Father.

You may be surprised by the lengths to which it is possible to go in unpacking a superficially simple story, but that, it seems to me, is what we do with stories, at any rate stories of the kind that we find in the Bible. They are not bare recitals of events, there to make us go, 'How amazing!' They are there to convey a level of truth that stark facts simply cannot do. That is not at all to say that these stories may not be based on factual events, but that they are much more than that. To reject what these stories say to us because we are still trying to decide whether or not we are reading precise factual accounts of events is futile. Better by far to imagine ourselves in a small, hot room in Ephesus or Corinth or Rome, hearing the story told to us for the first time, to let our imagination take wing, to capture the excitement and awe of the narrative and identify, if we can, with the experience of the characters taking part in it: that is the sheer wonder of the story and that is its timeless power to convey truth. And that, I would suggest, is why so much of the Bible is told in the form of stories.

4
The Bible and Ethics

'Go and find out what Johnny's doing, and if he's enjoying it, tell him to stop!' That's how many people think of religious believers: killjoy puritans with grim faces and black Bibles under their arms. Often the only occasions when the general public becomes aware of Christians are, unfortunately, when they're protesting against something: abortion, homosexuality, a march in Northern Ireland.

These impressions are often reinforced by figures in television soap operas and cartoons. Most of the Christians depicted seem to be either narrow-minded prigs or cheerful hypocrites. Think of Ned Flanders in *The Simpsons*, for instance. Some caricatures have elements of cruel truth, of course, but anyone who has even a passing acquaintance with most churches will know that that is by no means the whole story, just as it simply isn't true that most, or even many, Christians join in protests against the sort of things I've mentioned. By far the biggest recent Christian 'protests' have been concerning war, or the cancellation of debt for poor countries – but that doesn't alter the deep-seated preconception about Christians and morality.

Pages of Prohibitions

Ideas like these also tend to colour people's approach to the Bible itself, so that it is assumed that within its solemn binding there are pages and pages of prohibitions backed up by quite horrible sanctions.

In fact, that's not entirely so. It's true that the Law of Moses, a central element of the Jewish tradition, occupies the best part of three books of the Old Testament, and it does contain many prohibitions and sanctions, some of them drastic ones. The so-called

'Wisdom' literature – Proverbs and Ecclesiastes – offers down-to-earth advice on right living, but few 'prohibitions'. Among the stories of Jesus there are several chapters of direct moral and ethical teaching, among them the famous 'Sermon on the Mount'. Far from being killjoy diatribes, however, they are profound reflections on the good life, balancing justice and mercy, right living and a reluctance to judge others. In much the same way, in his letters to the emerging churches of the first century the apostle Paul offers moral and ethical teaching, though always presented in the context of the Christian message of forgiveness and grace. The same is true of the apostles James and Peter in their letters.

Taken as a whole, then, it would be untrue to say that the Bible is principally a book of prohibitions, though it does concern itself from first to last with the development of what we might call a 'godly character'; life lived in the way God intended for us. For anyone who wants to reflect on what a truly 'good' human life is and how to live well, which in our best moments I suppose all of us do, the Bible is a wonderful storehouse of treasures.

How We Make Moral Choices

The ethical teaching of the Bible tends to reflect all three of the usual ways in which human beings reach moral choices. We do what we're told – keep the rules. Or we think about the consequences – if I do this, what will happen? Or we ask ourselves what would be the choice of a good and honest person in these circumstances. To oversimplify it, the element of Law in the Bible tells us what the rules are. Its stories and allegories spell out the consequences of our actions. And its teachers and preachers present to us the possibility of 'right living', of being 'pure in heart', merciful and peace-loving. The essential element in the Bible, the 'added value', is of course the involvement of God, who is himself holy, righteous, merciful and good.

So there is certainly in the Bible a prominent vein of ethical teaching, and it is this element that we shall consider in this chapter. It is easily misread, usually by those who ignore its historical or cultural context, or who are thumbing through the Bible for simple answers to complex questions. For instance, it is true that there are in the Old Testament quite horrendous penalties laid down for what the Western world would nowadays regard as trivial offences, such

The Sermon on the Mount by Fra Angelico (c. 1395–1455),
from a monk's cell in the Convent of San Marco in Florence.

The Bible and Ethics

THE TEN COMMANDMENTS

The Ten Commandments (or 'Decalogue') are the heart of the Law that Israel received as a gift from God. It's often called the 'Mosaic Law' because it was Moses to whom it was given on Mount Sinai.

The Ten Commandments divide into two sections. The first three deal with our relationship to God; the last six with our relationship to each other. Between them, as a kind of transition, is a commandment about observing the Sabbath on the seventh day of the week – a day when no work was to be done, not even by slaves, resident aliens or livestock.

The first group of laws command worship of God alone, forbid any form of idolatry and warn that the sacred name is to be treated with reverence.

The final group cover universally recognized sins, such as murder, theft, deceit, marital disloyalty and two social flaws: failing to honour one's parents, and envy of the possessions of others.

as collecting twigs on the Sabbath day. Indeed, some of the Jewish Law is as severe as the Shari'a law which is applied in its most literal form in a few Muslim countries today – stoning for adultery, amputating hands, flogging and so on. Taken out of its historical context and simply seen as a universal or eternal expression of divine justice, it might lead the reader to dismiss the whole of the Bible, or even God himself, as barbaric. In fact, what we call the Law of Moses was clearly provided for an emerging people, a nation still in its birth throes, unsure of its own identity and under pressure from alien cultures and religions all around it.

Not surprisingly, it sounds harsh and unrelenting to us, with few escape routes or concessions to human failure. Any reading of it needs to be balanced with the many examples of God's mercy and kindness to be found in the Jewish Scriptures, especially in the Psalms and later prophets; an insight which reaches its height in the moral teaching of Jesus in the Gospels.

Is There a 'Biblical Ethic'?

Is there, then, nothing which could be called a 'biblical ethic'? There are two answers to this. The first is 'No,' because the Bible tells us the story of an emerging or developing understanding of the nature of God, moving from what might be called a simple or even primitive view to a more mature understanding. This is what is known as 'progressive revelation': the idea that the revelation of God in the Bible progresses from the simple to the complex, from a tribal deity to a universal Father, from the God of Abraham to the God and Father of Jesus.

The second possible answer is 'Yes,' because right from the start certain principles can be seen which apply to almost all of what we could call the ethical or moral teaching of the Bible.

The first and most important of these is the notion of Creator and creature. 'It is he who has made us, and not we ourselves,' as the psalmist said. God has created us in his own 'image', bearing many marks of his nature: creativity, self-consciousness, moral autonomy, love. If human beings, *all* human beings, are made in that image, then *all* human beings are of infinite value, and their lives should be treated with respect. Even at its most bloodthirsty, I think it is true to say that the Bible values human life: 'Whoever sheds human blood, by a human shall his blood be shed.' One of the great commandments says quite simply, 'You shall do no murder.' Another rules out 'covetousness', wanting what others possess; as the whole of the natural world is God's creation, we are to see ourselves as 'stewards' of its riches, not their owners.

'God Knows Best'

But our nature as creatures goes further than that. If we are God's creatures, then we are for ever dependent to some extent on him. This principle underlies much of the Bible's moral teaching. We might put it crudely by saying, 'God knows best.' It was defiance of that principle that led to rebellion in the Garden of Eden, as we have seen. Knowing, or thinking that we know, better than our Maker is a catalyst for disaster.

Another principle that undergirds biblical ethics is that of justice. 'Shall not the Judge of all the earth do what is just?' This rhetorical question was put to God by Abraham in the context of the sordid story of Sodom and Gomorrah (Genesis 18:25). He was

Blind Justice?

In the statue of Justice which stands above the Old Bailey law courts in London, 'Justice' is blindfolded – that is, impartial – and weighs out in her scales the rights and wrongs of a situation. In the Bible, justice is an attribute of God, but is generally balanced by his other fundamental characteristic, which is righteousness – 'Shall not the Judge of all the earth do what is just?' (Genesis 18:25).

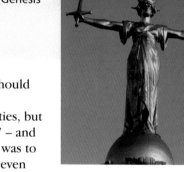

pleading that God should not slay the entire population of the cities, but spare the 'righteous' – and his eloquent appeal was to God's justice rather even than to his mercy. By his nature, the Bible assumes, God will do what is 'right'.

The Principle of Mercy

Yet another principle underlying biblical ethics is God's mercy. This is a great theme of the Psalms: though judgment is deserved, we receive mercy, and receive it as a gift, not something we can earn or deserve. Although the God of the early books of the Bible comes across as severe and awesome, even here there are continual hints of this 'other side' to his nature. He has mercy even on Cain, the first murderer, sparing his life and putting a 'mark' on him so that people finding him should not kill him out of hand (see Genesis 4:15). He shows mercy, time and again, to the cantankerous, moaning and sometimes downright rebellious Israelites on their long journey across the wilderness (see, for instance, Exodus 16:11, 12). God's mercy is blended with the idea of his love in the Hebrew word *hesedh*, translated very beautifully in the King James Bible as 'loving-kindness'. This idea is woven into the text of the Old Testament. However stern God may be, however demanding his standards and uncompromising his own moral purity, he is a God of loving-kindness.

Human Responsibility

Probably the greatest single emphasis of biblical ethics, however, is human responsibility. In a unique way, and implicit in our nature as persons, we are responsible for our actions. The God of the Bible pays human beings the ultimate compliment of regarding them as answerable for their actions, moral arbiters capable of making choices, but inevitably bearing the responsibility for their consequences.

It is this aspect of biblical ethics, I think, which causes modern people most difficulty. We wish to have the right to choose, but we are reluctant to take full responsibility for our choices.

This can be seen time and again in our response to actual situations. We wish to be independent, yet when things go wrong we feel that somebody should rescue us. We claim the right to indulge our feelings and our fancies, but are reluctant to accept that our behaviour sometimes has unpleasant consequences. Reaping what we sow is not a popular notion, and yet in many respects it is at the heart of creation itself: the 'way the world is', the way, believers would say, that its Creator has willed it to be – not as an ugly penalty, but as a sign of human dignity and personhood.

If we are *not* responsible for our actions, then we are either moral automata, driven by our basic instincts or random responses to situations, or we are morally neutral, recognizing no preference for 'good' and 'bad', or 'just' and 'unjust'. We can see the first position in such explanations of behaviour as, 'I don't know what came over me, but I stabbed her,' and the second in, 'I needed money for drugs, so when I saw this old girl with her handbag I just grabbed it.' One response is justified by instinct or the situation I find myself in, the second solely by my 'need'. Neither could be justified by any objective standards of justice or right action.

Responsibility is a Privilege

The Bible doesn't see human responsibility as a handicap but as a privilege, a mark of being human. To be punished for doing wrong is not, in this way of seeing things, humiliating but dignifying: it marks us out as different from the animals, bearing responsibility for our actions. Take that away, and we lose all dignity and simply become slaves of our desires or instincts. Recognize it, and we become, as one of the Psalms says, 'a little lower than angels, crowned with glory and honour'. The privilege of choice between right and wrong, between justice and injustice, is part of the inevitable price of being truly human, truly made 'in the image of God'.

So we can see coherent ethical and moral principles worked out in the Scriptures. They aren't set out in a neatly codified way, but are there to be found in both the Hebrew Scriptures – what we call the 'Old Testament' – and in the New Testament. We shall find them in story, poetry and teaching, and as we do we shall recognize how profoundly and fundamentally true they are to the instinctive longing of the human heart for justice. The toddler screams, 'It's not fair!' and the adult constantly appeals to 'justice'. Either the words mean something or they mean nothing. If we decide that they do correspond to some deep yearning of human nature, a universal longing for 'righteousness', then we shall be much more than halfway to understanding biblical ethics.

Making Difficult Choices

So much for the principle. What about the practice? How are these ideas of justice and right living expressed in the text of the Bible? How can people use them in practice to make the sometimes very difficult choices we all face from time to time? To offer an answer to that, I turn once again to specific examples, both from the Old and New Testaments.

The first is found in a rather sordid episode in the life of David, the greatest of Israel's kings. It is a classic example of the Bible's honesty in recounting the weaknesses as well as the strengths of its heroes. You can read it in 2 Samuel 11. The opening sentences of the story hint that David was rather remiss in absenting himself from the battlefields and sending his general Joab with his officers to tackle the menace of the Ammonite army, preferring to remain in the comfort and safety of the capital. While his army is thus engaged, the king is found strolling on the roof of his palace, from which vantage point he sees a very beautiful woman bathing. He sends a servant to discover her identity, and learns that she is Bathsheba, the wife of Uriah, an officer in his army and consequently absent from home on active service. He sends for her to be brought to the palace and has sex with her; she would presumably have had little say in the matter. Some weeks later she sends a message to the king that she is pregnant with his child.

David's reputation as an honourable man is now at stake. He devises a scheme which is both clever and dishonourable. He sends word that Uriah shall be brought home from the battlefield, fed at the king's house and then encouraged to spend the night at home with his wife. Uriah comes to the palace, but declines David's suggestion about spending the night at home. 'The servants of my lord are camping in the open field; shall I then go to my house, to eat and drink and to lie with my wife? I will not do such a thing.' Thwarted, David tries getting him drunk. But still he will not go home to his wife.

In desperation, David sends a command to Joab to set Uriah in the forefront of the next battle and then to pull back the soldiers around him so that he would be killed in battle. The obedient Joab carries out his order to the letter and Uriah is slain. When Bathsheba hears of his death she goes into mourning, but as soon as the period of mourning is over David sends for her and takes her as a wife, thus making the baby to be born legitimate.

Murder and Adultery

The Bible coolly observes that what David had done 'displeased the Lord', and he sent the prophet Nathan to confront the king. Instead of charging him baldly with murder and adultery, which were his actual offences, Nathan recounted a story as though it were a current case. A rich man with many flocks and herds had a poor neighbour who owned only a single ewe lamb, which he had raised himself in his house. The rich man had a distinguished guest arrive unexpectedly and wished to kill a lamb for the feast. Instead of taking one from his own extensive flock, he stole the poor man's lamb, had it killed and prepared for the table.

David interrupted the story at this point in genuine indignation. 'The man who has done such a thing deserves death, and must also repay the loss fourfold from his own flock.' Nathan said very simply, 'You are the man' – and then outlined the divinely ordained penalty for his offence.

The story demonstrates very dramatically the principle of responsibility, even on the part of a king, and also the principle of justice. Put in terms of the simple case of the rich and poor neighbours, David could see the appalling injustice that was being done. With that particular blindness that afflicts all of us from time to time where our own faults are concerned, he did not see, until it was so forcefully brought home to him, that simply meeting his own desires without regard to justice or right behaviour was contrary to the fundamental moral principles of the world as God has made it.

In one way that is a very straightforward case of right and wrong, even if it took a good man a long while to see it.

Christ and the Woman Taken in Adultery by Bernardo Cavallino (1616–56).

Another story I have chosen, from the Gospels, is less obvious and straightforward, though it illustrates several of the principles of biblical ethics that have been outlined in this chapter. You can find it in John's Gospel, chapter 8.

The Woman Taken in Adultery

Jesus was teaching in the Temple precincts when members of what we would now probably call a fundamentalist sect of Judaism dragged a woman before him. 'This woman was caught in the very act of adultery,' they said. 'The Law of Moses requires that she be stoned to death. What do you say?' Jesus was silent, bending forward and 'writing with his finger on the ground' – though we're not told what he wrote. They repeated the question, and in the end he straightened up and said to them, 'Let anyone among you who is without sin be the first to throw a stone at her.' He then resumed writing on the ground. At this, they went away one by one, 'beginning with the elders', until Jesus was left completely alone with the woman. 'Where are they?' he asked the woman. 'Has no one condemned you?' She said, 'No one, sir.' He said, 'Neither do I condemn you. Go your way, and from now on do not sin again.'

Guilty, but Not Condemned

The contrast with the case of David is interesting. Both cases involve adultery, and in neither is the charge denied. They were unquestionably guilty. Yet in one case the Lord's prophet condemns and lays down the penalty, and in the other 'the Lord's prophet' – Jesus – declines to condemn and applies no penalty. The difference is not in the degree of the guilt, but in the circumstances.

David was clearly guilty of a serious abuse of power, and his adultery was compounded by what amounted to murder in an attempt to cover up his offence. We aren't told the circumstances of the woman's adultery – she may indeed have been a prostitute – but in any case the religious zealots had only applied half of the Law of Moses, which specifically says that *both* parties to the adultery were to be stoned, and it undeniably takes two people to commit adultery. Why had they omitted to bring the man to Jesus, one wonders; could it be because he had been employed by the enemies of Jesus in order to provide this opportunity to embarrass him and show him to be indeed what they alleged, a compromiser of the Law?

Whatever the case, and without, we may notice, in any way condoning her behaviour, Jesus weighed all the factors involved and decided that mercy and a warning would offer a better hope of reformation of character than the ultimate penalty which they demanded.

To Live Rightly

The principles both of the mercy of God and the responsibility of individuals for their actions seem to have been decisive in these two decisions. Taking into account all the biblical principles we have mentioned, we can see in these two cases the value placed on human life (Uriah's), the justice which goes far beyond simply applying a set of rules (the woman), the merciful nature of God (for in neither case was the ultimate penalty applied) and the responsibility of the individual (especially David's responsibility as the king). We can also glimpse here, perhaps, an even greater purpose: that the objective of morality and ethics, truly understood, is not the rule of law or even the avoidance of bad consequences, but the reformation of life. The aim is to live rightly and to help people to achieve that goal.

These two stories have been chosen because they illustrate several key principles of biblical ethics: human responsibility, the consequences of wrong choices, the principle of mercy and the ultimate purpose of reformation and renewal. What they obviously *can't* be taken as is 'case law'. Adultery is always wrong, but the appropriate corrective for it is not necessarily severe punishment; mercy is always good, but it cannot be used to evade the responsibility of judgment. God's will is greater than mere retribution and more subtle than blanket forgiveness.

The Sermon on the Mount

We shall find these principles worked out in far greater detail in the ethical teaching of Jesus, perhaps most clearly in the Sermon on the Mount (Matthew 5–7). The goal is nothing short of moral perfection: right character, or 'righteousness', as the Bible calls it. But throughout his teaching due regard is paid to human weakness, divine mercy, the value of forgiveness, and the

THE SERMON ON THE MOUNT

The Sermon on the Mount (Matthew chapters 5–7) brings together much of the teaching of Jesus on moral and ethical questions. It includes some of his best-known sayings, including 'Love your enemies' and 'where your treasure is, there will your heart be also'.

It begins with the so-called 'Beatitudes', a collection of sayings about what constitutes the 'good life', each one beginning 'Blessed (or happy) are...'

It ends with the well-known story of two men, one who built his house on rock, and the other who built on sand. The first stood firm under the impact of flood and storm. The second fell – 'and great was its fall!' Jesus explained that the 'rock' was his teaching, 'these words of mine'.

necessity of recognizing that justice is ultimately in the hands of God, not of humans. So the Law of Moses may sanction retaliation ('an eye for an eye'), though within strict legal controls, but Jesus rejects it as a right principle: 'Turn the other cheek... Go the second mile... Love your enemies, do good to those who treat you with scorn.' He is not now offering a legal code to order the life of an emerging nation, but a set of principles to guide the 'children of the kingdom of heaven'. Nothing he says contradicts the principles we have found running all through the teaching of the Bible, but they have now reached a new refinement in the teaching of Jesus. This is what we should expect if the principle of progressive revelation holds good: that as the story of God's relationship with the human race develops, so the picture becomes clearer. Christians would say that in Jesus it reached clarity, but that, of course, is a judgment of faith.

A Series of Case Studies

What we have seen, I would suggest, is that the Bible offers its readers a long series of case studies in applied ethics, in morality as it is lived rather than as it is set out in propositions. Some of the

Christ Teaching the Parable, from the parable of the Good Samaritan, Lancet Window at Chartres Cathedral, c. 1210.

case studies are, to the modern reader, quite repellent, and others fall outside our own experience of life. Behind them, however, lie those principles: our status as God's creatures, divine mercy, justice and human responsibility. Sometimes the emphasis seems to fall unduly on one rather than another, and sometimes the human perception of people or events seems to distort the picture. That, of course, is what we should expect if we are indeed reading the account of a long and sometimes disconnected journey; a journey of discovery in which God shows himself to us, and we try to understand what we are seeing.

The moral and ethical teaching of Jesus, for instance, is not, as some people suppose, in contradiction of the principles of right living that we discover in the Old Testament. Nothing he says goes beyond the magnificent words of the prophet Micah in the eighth century before Christ: 'What does the Lord require of you but to do justice, and to love kindness, and to walk humbly with your God?' In word and action, however, he applied them more radically than previous Jewish teachers. You could say that he drove them to their logical conclusions: if God is like this and if he requires this, then this is the sort of people we should try to be. The journey of spiritual discovery moves on, and arrives at a kind of resolution. And on the way, as we meet difficult moral choices from day to day, we may find that the teaching of the Bible, and especially of Jesus, will offer us a constant source of reference – not a list of rules, but a model to follow and a goal to pursue.

An Extraordinary Gentleness

Jesus allied commitment to the law of God with a degree of generosity, tolerance and kindness which some, at any rate, of the Hebrew prophets might have felt smacked of compromise. When faced with the poor, the helpless, the exploited, or with minority groups of the powerless (for example, women, in his day), or with those who were considered beyond the social and religious pale (such as Gentiles, collaborators with the Roman occupiers, lepers and the women of the streets), he exhibited a quite extraordinary gentleness and acceptance. At the same time, he was intolerant of power abused, of wealth indulged, of insincere religion. Where they were concerned, his language was forthright and his condemnation devastating. In Jesus 'righteousness' was not ugly or assertive, but neither was it weak and flabby.

A Shining New Perspective

As the first Christians struggled to apply these principles to their new lives of faith, they sometimes found the tension between law and grace difficult – a question the apostle Paul addressed at length in his demanding letter to the church at Rome. Yet from that community there began to appear a new kind of morality, which sought to do what was 'right' – to live the kind of life the Creator intended for us – without burdening itself with an enormous system of rules and law. Of course they sometimes failed, as Christians down the ages have often done. But when they got it right, or even nearly right – it was a shining new perspective on what might be meant by the 'good life'. 'Then the righteous,' said Jesus – those who seek to live as creatures in the Creator's world, doing what is right – 'the righteous shall shine like the sun in the kingdom of the Father'. I suspect that Moses, Elijah, all the great prophets and lawgivers of Israel, would say 'amen' to that.

5
Heroes and Villains

Which are the goodies, and which are the baddies? That's the sort of question my grandchildren might ask when settling down to watch a television programme or a pantomime. Heroes and villains are the stuff of fairy tales, and the great, legendary ones give us simple working models of good and evil: Superman and Lex Luther, Snow White and the evil Queen, Frodo Baggins and Sauron, and so on.

Do the heroes and villains of the Bible fall into the same category? Certainly the names are often included in any roll-call of such figures: David and Goliath, Samson and Delilah, even Jesus and Judas Iscariot. Does this mean that they too, or at least some of them, are simply legendary working models of good and evil lifestyles?

Again, there's no simple or categorical answer, if only because these characters are not entirely comparable. The Samson story is part of the saga of early Israel, and the marks of that literary form shape the narrative. David and Goliath are figures from recorded history, in one sense (I don't think anyone seriously suggests that David never existed or was never king of Israel), but their story has about it some 'legendary' qualities. I'm thinking of the details of the story: the armour David couldn't wear because it didn't fit, the smooth stones from a brook, the boasting of Goliath and, of course, his elevation from merely being a very tall man (which is how the Bible actually depicts him) to the status of a fully-fledged giant.

Jesus and Judas clearly fall into a different category. For one thing, we are much nearer the event and we have witnesses whose evidence was first documented well within the lifetimes of those involved. Though the Gospel writers undeniably cast Judas in the role of the villain, the companion and confidant who betrayed his friend for money, the setting is such that there is a complexity to the story and to his character that seems to move him beyond simple 'villainy'. For instance, Mark tells us that it was immediately after Jesus had spoken of being 'anointed for his burial' that Judas 'went

In the panoply of human heroes and villains it's easy to pick the real 'baddies', such as Saddam Hussein, and the real 'goodies', such as Mother Teresa of Calcutta. However, most people are not so easily categorized, and that certainly applies to the Bible's main characters, most of whom are either mostly good and occasionally bad, or vice versa.

We might think of Abraham under the first category. Undoubtedly a God-fearing man, he also exhibited fear of a less commendable kind when he and his 'very beautiful' wife Sarah went to Egypt during a time of famine. He was afraid that the Egyptians would kill him in order to take his wife, so he passed her off as his sister – with disastrous consequences for everyone (Genesis 12:10–20).

For the second category we might choose Pontius Pilate, prefect of Judea during the ministry of Jesus. History tells us that he was a cruel man who was finally stripped of his position because of his brutality. However, the Gospels show him as at least superficially sympathetic to Jesus at his trial, insisting that he could find 'no fault in him', and he insisted that the accusation written over his head should state baldly that he was 'Jesus of Nazareth, king of the Jews'. When the chief priests objected, Pilate simply answered, 'What I have written I have written' (John 19:21, 22).

to the chief priests in order to betray him to them' (Mark 14:9, 10). Could it have been that this was for him the last straw – Jesus turning his back on his true role as the Messiah, the Saviour of Israel, and instead accepting defeat and death at the hands of the authorities? It would seem that, almost reluctantly, the Gospel writers can't resist showing us a more complex betrayer than a man who simply did it for thirty pieces of silver.

An original approach to combating antisocial behaviour is shown on these billboards from Mexico City. Prominent figures such as Mother Teresa and Saddam Hussein, who represent good and evil, are used to grab the attention of passers-by.

Vivid Characters

In fact, it is impossible to read the Bible without being aware that its story is built around vivid characters, some inclined to the heroic, some to the villainous. Right from the start, as we have seen, we begin to meet these people: Adam and Eve, Cain and Abel, Noah and his sceptical neighbours and then Abraham and Sarah, Isaac and Jacob, and so on. Because it's impossible to get into the Bible or appreciate its message without considering them, this chapter offers a swift guide to the heroes and villains of the book, its *dramatis personae*, as we might say.

Adam and Eve

I have already mentioned Adam and Eve, whose names literally mean 'the man' and 'life', which suggests that they are perhaps representative rather than strictly historical. In any case, it would be hard, in human terms, to cast them as heroes or villains. They are more like characters in a sublime tragedy, who lose everything that is really good, true and worthwhile through a single moment of moral weakness or a single fallible element in their characters. It's too simple to say that they were 'good' and then became 'bad'. Perhaps the whole thrust of their story is to remind us that every human being walks a moral tightrope, that our words and actions often have unforeseen consequences, that there is a built-in penalty for living in a way that ignores or rejects the word and will of God.

Their elder son, Cain, is also a complicated case. He is correctly designated the first murderer in the biblical story, the first human being to shed the blood of another. But again it is too simple to say that he is 'just a villain'. It seems – the story is so briefly told that it is hard to judge – that he was envious of his brother's offering to the Lord, which was an animal sacrifice, and felt that his own offering from the crops was regarded as inferior. This may reflect later Jewish ritual practice, of course. In this story, however, it led to a fit of jealous anger in which Cain killed his brother Abel. That was an undeniably evil act, of course, and his penalty was in effect banishment from the human community – though not, interestingly, death. Indeed, the Lord 'put a mark on Cain's forehead' (the legendary 'mark of Cain') – 'so that no one who came upon him would kill him'. It was not so much an act of judgment as of mercy.

Abraham, David and Solomon

As we go on through the Old Testament we shall find that many of its most colourful characters also refuse to fit neatly into a 'hero' or 'villain' category. Abraham was in most respects heroic, leaving his home in Ur to travel westwards in response to a divine prompting, and determined to obey the Unseen God whatever he asked him to do. Yet while travelling towards the Negeb, Abraham engaged in a sordid and cowardly ruse to save his own skin, apparently preferring that the local ruler should think his wife Sarah was his

KING DAVID

David was the greatest king of Israel, and yet he is revealed in the Bible as on one occasion an adulterer who was prepared to arrange for the killing of the husband of the woman he wanted. David was the second of the kings of Judah, coming to the throne in the eleventh century BC after the death of Saul. He captured Jerusalem, bought the site on which the Temple was eventually built by his son Solomon, and created a united kingdom of the twelve tribes which was a major force in the world of the time. After Solomon's death the kingdom divided into the northern tribes, Judah, and the southern ones, Israel.

David combined many of the attributes that were to shape the Jewish vision of kingship. He had been a shepherd, and was seen as the one who would lead, protect and care for his people. He was anointed by Samuel, set apart for his solemn responsibilities. He was a great warrior, overcoming many of the nation's traditional enemies and creating for the first time a national sense of pride and worth. He was a man of profound faith, who may well have composed a number of the psalms in the psalter which became known as the 'Psalms of David', yet he also exhibited human frailty and moral failure. In the developing religion of Israel he was seen as a messianic figure, and the hope and expectation was that eventually a descendant of his would restore the kingdom to its former glory.

The tomb of King David on Mount Zion, Jerusalem, is still a place of pilgrimage for Jews and Christians to this day.

sister, and take her sexually, to telling the truth and risking the king simply killing him and taking Sarah as a concubine. You can read of the incident in Genesis 20:1–11.

This story, told without embellishment or excuse, is typical of the way in which the Hebrew Scriptures report the lives of their great men and women. Without exception, these are definitely 'warts and all' portraits. Samson's legendary strength is matched by his weakness for women, notably the scheming Delilah. David's moral failure over his affair with Bathsheba, which we have already considered (2 Samuel 11:1–27), offers a candid insight into the life of the one whom the Bible describes as 'a man after God's own heart'. We have Solomon the Wise showing questionable wisdom in acquiring an enormous harem of foreign women, numbering no less than a thousand wives and concubines, who were inevitably to 'lead him astray' (1 Kings 11:1–6). Then there is Elijah's fit of self-pity and cowardice during the reign of the notorious King Ahab, which led him to flee and hide in the desert until God ordered him back on duty (1 Kings 19:1–18). Abraham, David, Solomon and Elijah are towering figures in the Hebrew Scriptures: there are no greater men in the history of Israel. Yet the Bible ruthlessly exposes their human fallibility. Add to that the failures of many lesser figures in the great pantheon of faith and we have ample evidence of a determination on the part of the chroniclers to present the picture whole.

New Testament Characters

When one turns to the New Testament, it is equally obvious that the writers are determined not to be accused of adorning the truth. Great apostles like Peter and Paul are shown to have their full share of human weaknesses. Peter's famous denial that he even knew Jesus, let alone was one of his disciples, is given most prominence in the very Gospel, Mark, which is believed to draw on him as a primary source. Only there are we told that in denying any connection with Jesus he backed up his claim with an oath (Mark 14:71). Peter and Paul, these two figurehead leaders of the early church, are seen falling out over the issue of Jewish food practices (Galatians 2:11–14). Paul is found apologizing for a verbal attack on the high priest (Acts 23:3), and admits in his letter to the church at Corinth that he may be boasting too much about his authority (2 Corinthians 10:8). He also fell out with his gentle friend and first supporter, Barnabas, over the question of taking Mark with them on their second missionary journey (Acts 9:27 and 15:38–40), though later in his life he was eager for Mark to join him (2 Timothy 4:11). The last chapter of 2 Timothy shows us Paul in what sounds like a self-pitying mood (though the circumstances of his house arrest might be considered ample justification for it).

The first witness to the resurrection of Jesus is named as Mary Magdalene in all four Gospels, yet we also read that she was someone out of whom Jesus had cast 'seven demons' (Mark 16:9). She was probably not the reformed prostitute featured in medieval art, but was certainly not a 'respectable' member of society. Even the family of Jesus, presumably including his mother Mary, on one occasion attempted to restrain him from his public ministry, which had led people to claim he was 'out of his mind' (Mark 3:21). As we have seen, one of Jesus's chosen 'twelve', his closest male companions, was to betray him – Judas. Another, Thomas, at first refused to accept the evidence of the others for the resurrection, demanding to see and touch the risen Jesus for himself. The writers spare no one. Indeed, far from painting an idyllic picture of the early church, they offer us a scenario all too familiar to present-day church members: sexual scandal, financial fiddling, squabbles and rows.

The Unscathed Man

All of which makes the portrait of Jesus in the Gospels even more telling. Alone of all the great figures of the Bible, he seems to emerge unscathed from this moral searchlight. That does not mean that the Bible's picture of him is of a person living on a different plane from the rest of us. He is seen as having intensely human feelings and needs. On the eve of the crucifixion we find him in agony in the Garden of Gethsemane, pleading with his Father to spare him the ordeal that lay ahead – 'if it be possible'. He could certainly display anger in the cause of justice, driving the traders from the Temple courts and overturning their tables. Yet the picture we gain of him is of a man at peace with himself, with his environment and with his God, a person of truth and integrity. That is presumably why he stands tall even among the spiritual giants of the Bible and, indeed, in the annals of the human race.

If the Bible is largely a book about people and their stories, as I have argued, then those coming to it need only one essential commentary on it: their own experiences of human life. This is truly a People's Book: a book by people, about people, and for people. All the rest, as someone has said, is interpretation.

6

The Gospels: Biography with Bite

About three-quarters of the way through the Bible you come to what is for Christian readers its heart, the four books which are called 'Gospels'. The word – from middle English – simply means 'good news' and the books set out to tell the story of the life of Jesus of Nazareth. Together they provide most of the material on which we base our knowledge of the founder of Christianity.

Why Four Gospels?

It's reasonable to ask why we should need *four* such books, especially as three of them (Matthew, Mark and Luke) include so much identical material. That can be answered in two ways. Practically, the early years of Christianity saw a profusion of 'Gospels' and collected sayings of Jesus. The four we now find in our Bibles, Matthew, Mark, Luke and John, are the four which experience, the test of time and, one might claim, the wisdom of the church decided were the most authentic records of the life of Jesus.

The second answer is that the four books we have, for all their similarities, offer quite distinctive insights into his significance. The same material differently presented and with altered emphasis can help to fill out the portrait of a man who clearly made an enormous impact on those who knew him. So, while Mark, Matthew and Luke share whole tracts of the same narrative, each organizes it in such a way as to offer a slightly different perspective on Jesus. It is only when we see the picture whole, from these different angles, that we can begin to recognize the true stature and significance of the prophet from Nazareth.

Of course there is an added value in having four Gospels – they each add to the evidence, as it were. I remember a retired police superintendent listening to a group discussing the different Gospel accounts of the resurrection of Jesus and getting quite worried about the discrepancies between the stories. Eventually he intervened. 'As a policeman,' he said, 'I soon learned that if four people gave you exactly the same account of what they had seen there was only one conclusion to draw – collusion!' Having four Gospels, telling fundamentally the same story from different angles, gives greater credence to the whole case.

A Matter of History

Jesus was born during the reign of Herod the Great, who died in 4 BC, which straightaway tells us that those who drew up our calendar got the dates wrong! In fact, when the 2000th anniversary of the 'birth of Christ' was celebrated at the millennium the whole world was at least four years late. Most scholars would date his birth between 6 and 4 BC. He entered the public scene in the Jordan Valley and then on the shores of Lake Galilee about thirty years later, according to the third Gospel, Luke. Jesus was executed by crucifixion during the consulship of Pontius Pilate – almost certainly in the year AD 30 or within the next couple of years. Dates are notoriously hard to establish when conflicting calendars are in use, but Luke helpfully does his best to date the appearance of John the Baptist in the Jordan Valley at more or less the time that Jesus entered the scene. He places that event in the fifteenth year of the reign of Emperor Tiberius, which was probably AD 27.

It's worthwhile starting with such dates, because a chief preoccupation of the Gospels is to place the life of Jesus firmly in a historical setting. The Christian church, of which the four authors were members, owed its very existence to that historical fact, and Christian belief was emphatically based on the claim that 'Jesus Christ came in the flesh' (1 John 4:2) – that is, was physically present in the world, not a divine manifestation or heavenly being just assuming human form, like the 'gods' of the Greeks and Romans.

In fact, hardly any sane person nowadays would care to argue that Jesus of Nazareth never existed, his life, deeds or influence being recorded in many non-Christian sources, from the Jewish historian Josephus to the Roman writer Tacitus.

Are They 'Biographies'?

I have said that the Gospels set out to tell the story of Jesus, but that should not lead us to approach them simply as biographies in the modern sense. A modern biography tends to be an in-depth account not only of what the subject did or wrote, but also to offer some kind of assessment of the significance of his or her life as a whole. It will also try to put the person into historical context and offer copious evidence to back up its claims. Before we start to read it, we shall probably have some idea whether the writer is likely to be sympathetic or hostile to the subject. When we finally put the book down, we may well feel that we now know as much about the author of the biography as we do about its subject. Few biographies, in other words, are totally neutral, and they would probably be pretty boring if they were. Among writers it is well known that writing a major biography of someone, even a person usually regarded as villainous, tends to leave the author somewhat more sympathetic to them than before they started.

Some biographies are of living people, but probably the best ones are posthumous, because time gives its own perspective to a life. Indeed, some of the really great biographies of recent years – I think of Claire Tomalin's magnificent work on Samuel Pepys – are written many centuries after the event.

The Gospels are in some respects like modern biographies and in others radically different, and before taking a closer look at each of them it may be a good idea to ask why. They were, of course, all posthumous. The earliest, Mark, was probably written in the seventh decade of the first century, roughly thirty-five years after the crucifixion of Jesus. The last is generally (though not universally) reckoned to be John, which may well have been completed just before the end of the century – still less than seventy years after the death of Jesus.

It's interesting to put those facts into a modern perspective. A present day biographer of Lord Montgomery of Alamein, for instance, would be writing roughly sixty years after the 'event', the great battle that he took for his title. The Gospel writer Mark was twenty-five years nearer to the 'Jesus event' than that – not much time, really, for legendary or miraculous accretions to infiltrate the story. The apostle Paul, writing to the church at Corinth ten years before Mark's Gospel appeared, claimed that 'most' of the witnesses of the risen Jesus were still alive at that moment (see 1 Corinthians 15:6). Given that many of the closest associates of Jesus were either his own age or younger

– that's to say, under thirty when he died – that's not very surprising. They would have been in their fifties as Paul was dictating his letter in the year AD 54.

Passionate and Urgent Messages

In those respects, the Gospels are like many of the biographies on the shelves of our bookshops and libraries. However, all of the Gospel writers had one over-arching aim, which the last of them, John, put into unambiguous words. '(This) is written so that you may come to believe that Jesus is the Messiah, the Son of God, and that through believing you may have life in his name' (John 20:31). These books are not, in other words, cool, dispassionate, neutral accounts of the life of Jesus, to be analyzed and picked over by future scholars, but passionate and urgent messages to their readers, to be accepted and believed, with life-changing consequences. They were themselves believers in Jesus, and they wanted their readers to share what they had found through him. It is that element that gives these books their extraordinary sense of urgency and also gravity. This is life-or-death stuff!

Does this mean that the writers abandoned all pretence at factual accuracy? Are these documents simply propaganda? Are they so besotted with the person and message of Jesus that they have abandoned the normal standards of honesty that we should expect of anyone writing a serious account of an important and influential man, in order to win followers for his cause?

I believe that the answer to each of those questions is a firm 'no', as I shall try to demonstrate, but nevertheless the reader needs to have the issue in mind as they turn to the Gospels. To do otherwise would in fact be to emasculate them. We read them for the urgency of the message of Jesus, for a picture of a life that has had an unparalleled impact on the history of the world and for an insight into the meaning of both the message and the life for those who read their words today. That is why they were written – honest books, I believe, by honest men, with an honestly confessed purpose: we want to convince you!

An 'Orderly Account'

We have seen how John explained his purpose in the writing of his Gospel. Here is how Luke tells us his, and it is rather nearer the idea of biography that we usually encounter today. 'Since many have undertaken to set down an orderly account of the events that

CAPERNAUM

Capernaum, on the northern shore of the Sea of Galilee, was a centre for the ministry of Jesus in Galilee, enabling him to get by boat to the territories to the east of the lake and also to the towns and villages along the western shores. Galilee, in his day, was a separate province from Judea, with a substantial population of Gentiles who had settled there – giving it its 'nickname', 'Galilee of the Gentiles'. Galileans had a distinctive accent (see Mark 14:70) and lifestyle, many of them earning their living from the lake itself, through fishing. Jesus was born in Bethlehem, in Judea (a few miles from Jerusalem) but his hometown was Nazareth in Galilee, where his father was a carpenter.

Aerial view of Capernaum, on the northern shore of the Sea of Galilee.

have been fulfilled among us, just as they were handed on to us by those who from the beginning were eyewitnesses and servants of the word, I too decided, after investigating everything carefully from the very first, to write an orderly account for you, most excellent Theophilus, so that you may know the truth concerning the things about which you have been instructed' (Luke 1:1–4).

The reference to 'instruction' was presumably to the teaching which 'Theophilus', whoever he was, had received prior to his baptism. Apart from that, the intention is absolutely clear. Luke has set out to do what any decent biographer would do – to get back to primary sources, to sift the material, to arrange it in an orderly way into a book. Even here, however, we may notice the note of persuasion: 'so that you may know the truth'. There was more at stake for 'Theophilus', and for us, than simply getting the facts right.

The Authors

Having looked a little at the particular genre of literature with which we are dealing in the Gospels – what we might call biography with bite – it may be time to look more closely at the writers and the

different approaches which they took to their work. Mark may be the first historically, but for good reason Matthew has always been placed first in the list of the Gospels.

Matthew

I say 'with good reason' because he is evidently a link with what has gone before in the Bible – the Hebrew Scriptures, what Christians call the 'Old Testament'. His book begins with a lengthy genealogy tracing the family tree of Jesus all the way back to Abraham, the father of the Jewish race. This was a customary way to start an account of the life of a distinguished person, and there was no great need for it to correspond to hard biological fact. This is just as well in Matthew's case, because the whole argument rests on Joseph, 'the father of Jesus', whom he is shortly to tell us *wasn't* his father in a biological sense at all. Perhaps that's why he is carefully listed as 'the husband of Mary, of whom Jesus was born'.

This linking of the story of Jesus with the story of the Jewish people is to become a constant theme throughout the book. At least fifteen times in his Gospel something is said to have been done 'to fulfil what had been spoken through the prophets', and on other occasions it is made clear, without recourse to this particular verbal formula, that actions or words of Jesus were in fulfilment of an Old Testament prophecy.

If anyone were to read the Bible straight through from cover to cover – an interesting but extremely demanding way to tackle the book, it must be said – they wouldn't feel a quantum leap between the last chapters of the Old Testament, where Malachi speaks of the 'messenger' who will 'go before the Lord' and of the Lord himself 'suddenly coming to his temple', and the book of Matthew, where precisely those things are described. John the Baptist, the prophesied 'messenger', makes his appearance immediately after the nativity story, duly credited as fulfilling the words of the prophet Isaiah, and later on Jesus himself comes to the Temple and ritually 'cleanses' it (Matthew 21:12,13).

Matthew's Gospel is so steeped in the language and imagery of the Hebrew Scriptures that it has to be a reasonable assumption that it is written by a Jewish Christian in a Jewish setting. In the first persecution of the church, in the very early days, most of the believers were 'scattered' to the districts surrounding Jerusalem, where the Temple authorities had less direct influence. A church remained in the city, however, presided over by the apostle James, until he too was taken and executed. Matthew's Gospel is generally reckoned to include the records – written and oral – of that Jerusalem church, and to have been compiled in a Hebrew rather than a Greek setting.

Sayings of Jesus

There is a mention attributed to Papias, bishop of Hierapolis in the first half of the second century, of 'Matthew' compiling *logia* (probably 'sayings') in 'Hebrew', which the early church took to refer to material for this Gospel. If these were 'sayings' of Jesus it would perhaps account for some of the material in this Gospel which isn't found in any of the others – mostly, as we might expect, to do with the refutation by Jesus of claims to authority by the Jewish rabbis and teachers of his time. 'Hebrew', incidentally, must be taken to mean Aramaic, which was the language of Jesus and the Jewish people of his time.

This raises the question of the authorship of the Gospels. In fact, all of them are anonymous, in the sense that the actual text in no case provides us with an author's name. Matthew's name – possibly for the reason already mentioned – was attached to the first Gospel from the earliest times.

He is listed as one of the disciples of Jesus, indeed one of the chosen 'twelve' who were his closest companions and to whom he imparted his teaching most intimately. According to the Gospels themselves he had been a 'tax-collector' for the hated Roman occupying authority, so would have been a figure of scorn among his fellow Jews. When he met Jesus, however, he 'left the tax booth' and followed him. His Gospel – if indeed he is its author – draws heavily on both Mark's and Luke's for much of its material, only about 35 per cent being unique to this book. As we shall see, that degree of 'duplication' of material is common in the first three Gospels, which are often called for that reason the 'synoptic' Gospels (because they look at the story through the same 'eye'). It must be said, however, that if Matthew the apostle was in fact the author of this Gospel it is strange that he should feel the need to rely quite so heavily on the writings of two men who were *not* apostles, and in the case of Luke were not even Jews.

A 'Jewish' Gospel

This is generally regarded as the most 'Jewish' of the Gospels, and its author as evidently himself a Jew. There is much internal evidence for this – Jewish names and phrases untranslated and

THE GARDEN TOMB IN JERUSALEM

The 'Garden Tomb' in Jerusalem is located at the site of what is known as 'Gordon's Calvary', after General Gordon, who first suggested this rocky outcrop and the garden below it as possible sites for the crucifixion and burial of Jesus. It is now generally accepted that this could not have been the actual site, because in the first century it was within the city walls, thus contradicting the biblical narratives. However, this is an excellent specimen of a genuine first-century tomb, and enables visitors to visualize the way in which Jesus was buried, with a heavy stone rolled across the entrance.

Most scholars accept that the actual site of Golgotha ('Calvary', in Latin) now lies under the Church of the Holy Sepulchre in the modern city – though in the first century it would have been outside the walls. Once one has penetrated the various objects of devotion and altars of the rival Christian denominations who share the building, it is possible to visit a first-century tomb underneath a rocky mound – the probable site of the crucifixion of Jesus.

The entrance to
the 'Garden Tomb',
Jerusalem.

unexplained (*raka* in 5:22 and *korbanos* in 27:6), Jewish religious practices, like ritual hand-washing, taken for granted. Matthew changes the usual 'kingdom of God' in the other Gospels to 'kingdom of heaven', thus, in Jewish style, avoiding unnecessary reference to the sacred name. He alone of the Gospels speaks of Jesus' mission as to 'the lost sheep of the house of Israel' and he alone has nothing good to say about the Samaritans, who generally get a good press in the New Testament although they were widely despised by Jewish people as defilers of the true religion.

Despite all this, however, Matthew's Gospel, while certainly Jewish in tone, is in many ways the most 'anti-Jewish' of the synoptic Gospels. Unlike the others, he is not content to demonstrate how Jesus came as the Saviour of the whole world (though that is, in fact, another clear emphasis of this Gospel) but that his coming is also a fearful judgment on the Jewish people, who have failed to recognize, and finally rejected, their Messiah. In this Gospel the denunciation of the Temple leadership, the scribes (the 'teachers of the Law') and of the religious sect of the Pharisees is especially scathing. The evidence suggests that this book was written during the period of the first severe rift between the emerging church and the synagogues and consequently in places reads like a piece of Christian polemic.

This seems consistent with the idea of a Jewish author or compiler, for whom the rift between the two ways would have been personally painful. It's well known that the most fervent campaigners for a cause are recent converts to it, and Matthew may well fall into that category. Certainly, in common with the other Gospel writers, he wants to argue with all the evidence he can muster that Jesus is the long promised Messiah ('Christ', in Greek). Despite that, he is more cautious than the other authors in putting that claim into the mouth of Jesus himself, preferring to let others come to that conclusion and testify to it. The most dramatic example would be the dialogue on the road to Caesarea Philippi (Matthew 16:13–17).

For Matthew, the preferred title of Jesus is the one constantly on the Lord's lips, 'the Son of Man' – a pleasantly ambiguous one with genuine roots in the Hebrew Scriptures (see, for instance, Daniel 7:13).

Mark

The second Gospel in our Bibles is Mark, though actually it was almost certainly the first Gospel to be written. A strong tradition, and some internal evidence, links its authorship with the young man John Mark who appears in the book of Acts at his mother's home in

Jerusalem soon after the crucifixion, and may well be the unnamed 'young man' who escaped naked from the scene when Jesus was arrested (Mark 14:51–52). Later he travelled with the apostle Paul on one of his missionary journeys. He failed to please his rather demanding leader, and Paul declined to take him on a subsequent mission. However, a reference in one of Paul's letters suggests that they were later on warm and friendly terms again (see Acts 15:36–40 and 2 Timothy 4:11).

There is a strong tradition that he ended up in Rome, where his Gospel was compiled, possibly with the apostle Peter as a primary source (again, internal evidence supports that – incidents and details that only Peter would have known). The general view is that it was written around AD 65–70. It is short compared to the other three Gospels and moves at a brisk pace – Mark's favourite word is 'immediately', though most translations hide this by varying it with 'at once' or 'without delay'. This is a Gospel of stark brush strokes, a story of action – indeed, of a battle on a cosmic scale between the power of light and goodness in Jesus, and the darkness and evil of the unbelieving world. Almost all of Mark's material can also be found in Matthew and Luke, though arranged differently in terms of order and presentation.

A Frantic Pace

Mark's Gospel moves at a frantic rate. Story follows story at a breathless pace – just read chapter 1:21 to the end to see what I mean. Jesus teaches in the synagogue, casts out an unclean spirit, heals Simon's mother-in-law of a 'fever', and then after dark deals with a crowd of sick and sorry people who have gathered at the door of the house. He goes to bed, but gets up while it's still dark to pray in a private place, only to be hunted down by his disciples and told that 'everyone' is looking for him. He then leaves with them for the neighbouring towns, to preach and heal there. And all of this in the space of less than two days!

Mark's pace has a purpose. For him, the coming of Jesus signals the start of a cosmic struggle between the forces of evil and the agent of the light. That first miracle – the casting out of 'unclean spirits' – sets the tone for the whole book. There is a solemn tone of conflict all through the narrative, which reaches its peak in Mark's account of the arrest, trial and crucifixion of Jesus. It is all painted in the most sombre tones, the apparent victory of death and darkness. The dying Jesus gives a loud cry and 'breathes his last'. So much, the reader might feel, for the 'good news of Jesus Christ, the Son of God' which we were promised in the opening words of the Gospel.

A Dramatic Reversal

Then, however, in what is a remarkable *coup de théâtre*, Mark manages to turn the whole dismal story upside down. His account of the resurrection is much, much shorter than those in the other Gospels – a mere eight verses in the authentic text. Yet the message is dramatic and clear. The heavenly messenger at the empty tomb tells the women, 'You are looking for Jesus of Nazareth, who was crucified. He has been raised; he is not here.' There is no elaboration. That isn't Mark's style. For him, the drama is in the event itself. Death and darkness has not conquered. This is a story of 'good news'. Jesus really is the Messiah, the Son of God.

Luke

As we have seen, Luke, the author of the third Gospel, set out his approach to the task in the prologue to his book. His was to be an 'orderly' account based on eye-witness testimony. Indeed, he does offer more historical markers than the other writers, even if in one case he seems to have got his dates slightly muddled over the governorship of Quirinius (2:2). His Gospel is written in a much more polished literary style than the others, as befits a professional man – Paul tells us Luke was a 'physician'.

A Gifted Storyteller

In fact, he is clearly a gifted storyteller. In his hands parables come alive, their characters vivid and recognizable. Only he gives us the Good Samaritan and the Prodigal Son, both exquisitely related stories full of human interest. He seems to have a wry sense of humour – think of the story of the dishonest manager (16:1–9) and notice the lovely touches of detail in the dialogue, as well as the enigmatic ending to the tale. Or there is the parable of the talents, in which three servants are entrusted with ten, five and one talent respectively, and told by their master to use them to make a profit. The man with one talent did what cautious savers always do: he wrapped it in a cloth – the first century equivalent of hiding it under the mattress. When the moment of judgment came, he had the one talent taken off him and given to the one with ten. Only Luke gives us the comment of the crowd listening to Jesus' story: 'Lord, he's got ten already!'

A Concern for the 'Have-nots'

Luke offers us a Gentile's portrait of Jesus, but also that of a biographer determined to reveal aspects of the character of Jesus which the other writers tend to overlook. Luke constantly draws attention to the concern of Jesus for the have-nots, the social outcasts and the powerless. His is the Gospel for and about the poor, the racially despised, the 'humble and meek'. And his is *the* Gospel for women, who have an enormous and important role in it from first to last.

His Gospel might be seen as Paul's Gospel, because they were companions on some of the apostle's most demanding missionary journeys and 'only Luke is with me' during his final house arrest

THE SUPPER AT EMMAUS

This beautiful painting captures in a very powerful way the moment at which the risen Jesus, invited to share an evening meal with the two disconsolate disciples he had met on the road, gives thanks and breaks the bread. At that point, Luke tells us, 'their eyes were opened and they recognized him' (Luke 24:31). Forgetting how tired they were, and that it was now dark, they hurried back to Jerusalem to tell the other disciples what had happened, and how Jesus 'had been made known to them in the breaking of the bread' (v35).

The Supper at Emmaus by Michelangelo Merisi da Caravaggio (1573–1610).

(2 Timothy 4:11). Yet there is an openness about Luke's approach, especially to women, which Paul might well have secretly envied. When Luke speaks of his 'eye-witnesses' it is tempting to imagine that they included Mary the mother of Jesus, who in her later years lived at Ephesus, and presumably belonged to the church there which Luke (a native of the region) must surely have visited. If that is indeed so, it would lend great weight to his account of the birth of Jesus and to the only story of his boyhood preserved for us (Luke 2:41–51).

Luke includes much material common to Mark and Matthew, but most of that which is original consists of parables, post-resurrection appearances (including the beautiful story of the supper at Emmaus) and, of course, the births of John the Baptist and Jesus.

John

The fourth Gospel, John, is radically different from the other three, as will be immediately apparent to the reader. Matthew begins his story with Abraham, Luke with the birth of John the Baptist, Mark in the wilderness of Judea with the voice of the fore-runner ringing out the news. John takes us back to 'the beginning', the creation itself, with a magnificent prologue setting the incarnation – the appearing of God's Son as a human being – in the perspective of eternity.

He introduces the reader to the 'Word' – *logos*, in Greek – who was with God from the beginning and was himself divine. Through this Word everything was created and through him life itself came into being. The Word is also a light shining in the world's darkness, touching with its rays every human life and – as light is accustomed to do – always conquering darkness.

'The Word' and the World

The Word was 'in the world' but unrecognized by the world. Even 'his own people' – presumably the Jews – did not accept him, although those who *did* accept him were given the authority to become 'children of God'. Finally, having waited until verse 14, we find out who this 'Word' is. 'The Word became flesh and lived among us, and we have seen his glory, the glory as of a father's only son, full of grace and truth.' The Word, in short, is Jesus, who alone would make God fully known: 'It is God the only Son, who is close to the Father's heart, who has made him known.'

From the Prologue, which it is hard to think of as written by a Galilean fisherman like John, we move into more familiar territory with John the Baptist and the baptism by him of Jesus in the River Jordan. From there on the story has a familiar ring for those who have read the other Gospels, but always with a distinct difference of tone and approach. Only one of the miracles of Jesus is common to all four Gospels, the feeding of the five thousand. In any case, John doesn't call them 'miracles' but 'signs', evidences, revelations as to the true nature and meaning of Jesus. All through the fourth Gospel the reader will feel there is 'more to this than meets the eye', which is in fact the most important clue to its appreciation.

'More Than Meets the Eye'

There is indeed 'more than meets the eye', because John sees the story of Jesus through the faith experience of the early church. Although he alone omits any account of the last supper and the

Detail of *The Baptism of Christ* by Giotto di Bondone (c. 1267–1337).

institution of Holy Communion, his Gospel is profoundly sacramental. For him the feeding of the five thousand is all about Jesus as the 'bread of life', whose 'flesh is truly food' and whose blood is 'truly drink'. Nothing is in this Gospel simply because it 'happened'. It is there because it *mattered* and it tells us something unique about who Jesus is or why he came to earth.

A Unique Claim

In one sense the identity of the authors of the Gospels is not important. The books are in the Bible because they were judged worthy to stand alongside the other Scriptures as evidences of great truths. However, this Gospel makes a unique claim, that it is the testimony of one of the twelve apostles, indeed the one identified throughout this Gospel as 'the beloved disciple' (see John 21:24). Although he is never named, it doesn't require an Hercule Poirot to work out that he is in fact John, the brother of James and son of Zebedee (Mark 1:19,20).

Of course, if the book is indeed written by, or based on the testimony of such a person, it immediately acquires unique authority, which may be why from earliest times this has been regarded as the greatest of the Gospels.

We should probably not, however, read John for the most precise historical account of the life and sayings of Jesus, mainly because that was clearly not the writer's intention. This is the kind of biography that is the memoir of a close friend written long, long after the event. What it offers us is an astonishing insight into the impact that Jesus made on those closest to him. The words may not be verbatim transcripts of his speech, but they may be taken to convey with scrupulous honesty the *effect* that they had on their first hearers. No one knew Jesus, humanly speaking, better than John (except possibly his mother, of course). Here, in this Gospel, we have that knowledge distilled through discourse, sign and action. The 'beloved disciple' saw it all and treasured it in his heart. Decades later, filtered through the continuing experience of the life of the infant Church, he handed on to us this incomparable testimony. John the apostle may not have written down its actual words, but we may be confident that it conveys his own unique insight into the personality and impact of Jesus, even if someone else (perhaps one of his own 'disciples') acted as compiler or secretary for the task.

Approaching the Gospels

How should the modern reader approach the Gospels? One suggestion would be to start with the oldest and shortest, Mark, then to read Matthew to put the story into its context with the rest of the Bible. Having done that, you are ready for the cool and precise Dr Luke, with his eye for characters and stories but also, as we've seen, a desire to put it all into a historical setting. Finally, you can turn to the 'treat', John. Expect to be a bit baffled by him at times, but enjoy the seven 'signs' – miracles, the other Gospels call them – and the memorable sayings beginning with the words 'I am ...' 'I am the light of the world', 'I am the good shepherd', 'I am the way, the truth and the life', 'I am the vine, you are the branches', 'I am the bread of life', 'I am the resurrection and the life', and so on.

The Personality and Character of Jesus

Whatever else they are, the Gospels are not boring, and most readers coming to them freshly are bowled over by the personality and character of Jesus as they emerge from these pages. I remember, many years ago, inviting a young singer/actor who had been cast for the role of Jesus in *Jesus Christ Superstar* in the West End of London to read the four Gospels as background preparation. He had never read them before, certainly not as continuous narratives. The effect they had on him was, to put it mildly, radical.

That was precisely the intention of their writers. These are books designed to convince. They do not so much argue a case or even tell a story as offer evidence. Here are the witnesses to probably the most amazing and influential life that has ever been lived on this planet. Their story is worth the telling, and infinitely worth the reading.

7

Wisdom and Wise Sayings

Most ancient religious literature is full of 'wise sayings'. In fact, some religions – Confucianism, for instance – are based entirely on such teaching, the adherent setting out to live life according to the principles of the founder's wisdom. Halfway through the Old Testament we begin to encounter similar teaching, much of it ascribed to Solomon, King David's son and successor.

The Wisdom of Solomon

When Solomon came to the throne, the book of Samuel records, God told him he could ask of him whatever he liked. The new king asked for 'wisdom'. Because he hadn't asked for riches or length of days, the Lord was pleased and granted his request. From that time on Solomon's 'wisdom' was legendary, and it is of course preserved in our English saying 'the wisdom of Solomon'.

In fact, by normal criteria he doesn't seem to have been all that 'wise', making something of a mess of his marital situation and even dabbling

in the religious practices of the cultures surrounding Israel. Yet when the Queen of Sheba came to visit him she was amazed at the wealth of his kingdom and the wisdom with which he had governed it.

Wisdom Applied to Two Women

One or two stories of that wisdom being applied are noted in the Bible, the best known concerning two women – prostitutes – who brought a small baby to him, both claiming that it was theirs. Solomon had an answer. He ordered that the baby should be cut in two and each woman given half. At this, one of the women,

Solomon and the Queen of Sheba by Claude Vignon (1593–1670). The Queen of Sheba, ruler of the Sabean tribe in south-west Arabia, visited the court of King Solomon, possibly in the hope of developing commercial links with the growing economy of Israel. However, the lasting impression the visit made on her was of the king's 'wisdom' and wealth (1 Kings 10:1–9).

appalled at what was about to happen, said that the baby could be given to the other. Instead, Solomon decreed that she should have the baby, because her reaction had proved her to be the true mother (1 Kings 3:16–27). I suppose it's simpler than DNA testing!

Sanctified Common Sense

The book of Proverbs is described in its opening as 'the proverbs of Solomon son of David, king of Israel'. There follow literally hundreds of wise sayings, mostly in the form of Hebrew verse, with the addition of some fifty more sayings by 'Agur son of Jakeh' and King Lemuel, both probably rulers of the Massa tribe. Their inclusion shows that the Wisdom literature of other cultures could be readily incorporated into the biblical text, though it is probable that they were editorially amended to suit the style of the rest of the collection.

The sayings cover a vast range of topics. Some are widely known: 'Go to the ant, you sluggard; consider its ways and be wise.' Many are truly poetic, like these verses from the proverbs of Agur:

Three things are too wonderful for me;
Four I do not understand:
The way of an eagle in the sky,
The way of a snake on
* a rock,*
The way of a ship on
* the high seas,*
And the way of a man
* with a girl.*

'Go to the ant, you sluggard; consider its ways, and be wise.' So says the book of Proverbs (6:6), in a typical piece of down-to-earth wisdom.

From this you will gather that not all have any deep 'religious' message. In fact, many are what we might call sanctified common sense. Some are found difficult by modern Western people – 'Spare the rod and spoil the child', for instance – but most offer perceptive comments on human frailty and at the same time ways to demonstrate 'wisdom'.

Divine Wisdom

Behind these Jewish 'Wisdom' writings there lurks a hidden concept, a quality or value in wisdom which elevates it from simply being a category of writing to a kind of personification of the divine. There is a particular instance of this in the book of Proverbs (8:22–31), where 'Wisdom' is spoken of as the first of God's creative acts, and an assistant or co-worker in creation itself. Several times the Old Testament reminds its readers that 'the fear of the Lord is the beginning of wisdom', but this seems to go further than that. Wisdom was involved in the shaping of the mountains, the foundations of the earth, the soil, the sea and the mysterious waters.

This is probably no more than a poetic way of saying that God's wisdom is as characteristic of his nature as his holiness or his justice. God is wise. He knows and he understands. Our times and our destiny are entirely in his hands. If it is true that the one who 'knows' is always the one who has true power, then God, who knows everything, has absolute power.

Some Examples of Old Testament 'Wisdom'

Human beings are born to trouble, just as sparks fly upward. (Job 5:7)

If the Almighty is your gold and your precious silver, then you will delight in the Almighty and lift up your face to God. (Job 22:25,26)

Truly, the fear of the Lord, that is wisdom; and to depart from evil is understanding. (Job 28:28)

Trust in the Lord with all your heart, and do not rely on your own insight. In all your ways acknowledge him, and he will make straight your paths. (Proverbs 3:5,6)

The beginning of wisdom is this: Get wisdom, and whatever else you get, get insight. (Proverbs 4:7)

Rejoice in the wife of your youth, a lovely deer, a graceful doe. May her breasts satisfy you at all times; may you be intoxicated always by her love. (Proverbs 6:19,20)

Go to the ant, you sluggard; consider its ways, and be wise... *A little sleep, a little folding of the hands to rest, and poverty will come upon you like a robber, and want, like an armed warrior.* (Proverbs 6:6; 9–11)

Treasures gained by wickedness do not profit, but righteousness delivers from death. (Proverbs 10:2)

Fools think their own way is right, but the wise listen to advice. (Proverbs 12:15)

If the wise go to law with fools, there is ranting and ridicule without relief. (Proverbs 29:9)

A fool gives full vent to anger, but the wise quietly holds it back. (Proverbs 29:11)

Charm is deceitful, and beauty is vain, but a woman who fears the Lord is to be praised. (Proverbs 31:30)

For everything there is a season, and a time for every matter under heaven. (Ecclesiastes 3:1)

That which is, already has been; that which is to be already is; and God seeks out what has gone by. (Ecclesiastes 3:15)

Like the crackling of thorns under a pot, so is the laughter of fools. (Ecclesiastes 7:5)

Do not say, 'Why were the former days better than these?' For it is not from wisdom that you ask this. (Ecclesiastes 7:10)

Again I saw that under the sun the race is not to the swift, nor the battle to the strong, nor bread to the wise, nor riches to the intelligent, nor favour to the skilful; but time and chance happen to them all. (Ecclesiastes 9:11)

The quiet words of the wise are more to be heeded than the shouting of a ruler among fools. (Ecclesiastes 10:17)

Send out your bread upon the waters, for after many days you will get it back. (Ecclesiastes 11:1)

For the end of the matter; all has been heard. Fear God, and keep his commandments; for that is the whole duty of mankind. (Proverbs 12:13)

THE WISDOM OF THE YOUNG JESUS

When Jesus was twelve his parents took him up to Jerusalem to visit the Temple. This may have been to coincide with his bar-mitzvah. When the family left to go back to Nazareth, the boy Jesus stayed on without their knowledge, fascinated by the various teachers of the Law – 'listening to them, and asking them questions', so that 'all who heard him were amazed at his understanding and his answers' (Luke 2:46,47). When his parents eventually found him they were understandably angry, but the boy coolly replied that they should have expected to find him 'in my Father's house'.

Wisdom and Jesus

The apostle Paul calls Jesus 'the wisdom of God', which directly links him with the concept of wisdom which we have found in the Hebrew Scriptures. In fact, the opening prologue of John's Gospel, which we looked at in the previous chapter, makes the connection explicit. Proverbs claims that 'when he (God) marked out the foundations of the earth, then I (Wisdom) was beside him, like a master worker, and I was daily his delight' (Proverbs 8:29–30). We can compare that with the language of John's Gospel: 'All things came into being through him (Jesus, the 'Word'), and without him

not one thing came into being' (John 1:2). Later in the New Testament, a section of Paul's letter to the church at Colosse uses much the same language and imagery with reference to Jesus: 'In him (Jesus) all things in heaven and earth were created' (Colossians 1:16). As we have seen, 'wisdom' was much more than just a matter of character or attribute to the Old Testament writers, but rather more like a person – perhaps a kind of personification of an aspect of God. For the New Testament writers, Jesus had become that person, or perhaps we ought to say 'Person'.

Detail of *Christ Among the Doctors* by Bernardino Pinturicchio (c. 1452–1513).

There can be no doubt that the first Christians saw Jesus as the 'wisdom' of which the Old Testament spoke, though his was in many ways a new 'wisdom' for a new age. In his own teaching Jesus emerges as a man of remarkable wisdom, not only in his understanding of people and events but also in his revealing of secrets known only to God. Several times the Gospels record that the crowds were 'astonished at his wisdom, because he taught with authority, not like the scribes' (see, for example, Mark 6:2). What they recognized was that he didn't simply explain or apply existing law or wisdom, as their religious teachers did, but had the authority within himself to teach a new and unique understanding of the ways of God.

One of his most striking sayings on the subject of wisdom is in Matthew 11:25–27: 'At that time Jesus said, "I thank you, Father, Lord of heaven and earth, because you have hidden these things from the wise and the intelligent and have revealed them to infants; yes, Father, for such was your gracious will. All things have been handed over to me by my Father; and no one knows the Son except the Father, and no one knows the Father except the Son and anyone to whom the Son chooses to reveal him." '

These words may help us to understand why the apostle Paul made a crucial distinction between the 'wisdom of this world' and the 'wisdom of God'. The first leads people into pride and error. The latter – while often looking foolish to secular eyes – is a source of both power and wholeness ('salvation'). The apostle works this out in a powerful passage in his first letter to the church at Corinth (1:17–25).

'Truly, Truly' Sayings

In practical terms, the teaching of Jesus often picked up characteristics of the Wisdom sayings of the Old Testament, especially the prophets. He often related a parable or a story, but then drove its message home with a neat summary, introduced with the Greek words 'amen, amen' – 'truly, truly'. It was as though he was saying to his hearers: 'Here's the headlines. Remember them. Think about them. Repeat them to yourselves. Eventually, the meaning will become clear!'

A good example of this approach can be found in Matthew 19:16–24. The story is straightforward yet obviously full of problems for the disciples, who had always been taught and believed that riches and prosperity were a sign of God's blessing, not a barrier to entering the kingdom. Yet here was Jesus telling a rich man that those very riches, far from being a blessing, could exclude him from the kingdom. As the man who had raised the question went away 'grieving', Jesus used his 'truly, truly' formula to point up the spiritual truth behind what he had done. Here is the passage in full:

Then someone came to him and said, 'Teacher, what good deed must I do to have eternal life?' And he said to him, 'Why do you ask me about what is good? There is only one who is good. If you wish to enter into life, keep the commandments.' He said to him, 'Which ones?' And Jesus said, 'You shall not murder; You shall not commit adultery; You shall not steal; You shall not bear false witness; Honour your father and mother; also, You shall love your neighbour as yourself.' The young man said to him, 'I have kept all these; what do I still lack?' Jesus said to him, 'If you wish to be perfect, go, sell your possessions, and give the money to the poor, and you will have treasure in heaven; then come, follow me.' When the young man heard this word, he went away grieving, for he had many possessions.

Then Jesus said to his disciples, 'Truly I tell you, it will be hard for a rich person to enter the kingdom of heaven. Again I tell you, it is easier for a camel to go through the eye of a needle than for someone who is rich to enter the kingdom of God.'

Pithy Sayings

Not only does this show how Jesus used the pithy saying to summarize or drive home the argument, but it also demonstrates how close, on some occasions, his style of teaching was to that of the writers of the Old Testament Wisdom literature. In fact, he taught in the style of a Jewish rabbi of his time. He asked questions, and answered them. He loved irony and ridicule. His teaching was full of stories and anecdotes as well as short sayings that could easily be remembered, like the camel and the needle's eye in this passage.

The 'Huff and Puff' Test

There is one characteristic of the Gospels here that is worth noting. It's what one leading New Testament scholar, Richard France, has called the 'I'll huff and I'll puff' test. When you tell a child the story of the 'Three Little Pigs', the one thing that really identifies it as authentic is the recital of the refrain of the Big Bad Wolf when he approaches another of the pigs' houses: 'I'll huff and I'll puff and I'll blow your house down.' Leave that out, and you'll have a dissatisfied client!

In many of the stories in the Gospels of Matthew, Mark and Luke there is a similar phrase, common to all three accounts, presumably because when the narrative was simply handed on by word of mouth (what experts call the 'oral tradition') this was the bit they all remembered. So in the feeding of the five thousand the catch phrase is 'They all ate and were satisfied' – even John has that one, too. In the account of the transfiguration of Jesus (Mark 9:8) the three accounts vary quite a bit in detail but they all end with the same words: 'When they looked around, they saw no one with them, but only Jesus.'

Similarly, in the story of Jesus driving the traders out of the Temple (Mark 11:17), the three accounts vary slightly in detail but all end with Jesus' words of rebuke: 'My house shall be called a house of prayer, but you have made it a den of robbers.'

The Topic Phrase

This literary device can also be taken, I suppose, to indicate the key or topic phrase in each story – this is the thing we are to remember, rather like the 'amen, amen' sayings. In the story we have just examined, the same is true of the saying about the eye of the needle. You may forget the details of the story, but you never forget that wretched needle!

All of this emphasizes how effective a teacher Jesus was. Huge crowds came to hear him and, according to the Gospels, 'hung on his words'. Unlike the traditional religious teachers, Jesus was saying 'new things', even if he was presenting them in a traditionally Jewish way. He certainly knew the value of story – and of irony, too. Think of his ridiculous comparison of the man with a plank in his eye offering to help to remove a splinter from someone else's (Matthew 7:3–5).

Jewish Speech Mannerisms

Having worked in broadcasting with some very popular Jewish speakers, like Lionel Blue and the late Hugo Gryn, I am familiar with various 'devices' which are characteristic of their approach – answering a question with a question, for instance, or telling a story as an illustration but pointedly not applying it. The parallels with

Jesus the Teacher are obvious. He often countered a question with another question (see, for instance, Luke 20:1–4). Very often he would end one of his 'parables' – a story with a 'meaning' – without even hinting at its application, but with the phrase 'He who has ears to hear, let him hear'. It's as though he was saying, 'There's the story. Now, you work it out!'

Sometimes the 'wisdom' of Jesus closely reflects the style of the Hebrew proverbs. 'Can the blind lead the blind? Surely both will fall into the ditch?' 'Wisdom is justified by its children.' 'You can't put new wine in old bottles.' 'Are grapes gathered from thorns, or figs from thistles?... You will know them by their fruit.' We will miss much of the 'flavour' of Jesus the teacher if we fail to recognize that he was a Jew, standing firmly in the traditions of his culture – however much he felt that culture needed renewal. If you try to take the Jew out of Jesus, you end up with a pale shadow of the real man.

Some Examples of the Wisdom of Jesus

Blessed are the peace-makers, for they will be called children of God. (Matthew 5:9)

You are the salt of the earth; but if salt has lost its taste, how can its saltiness be restored? (Matthew 5:13)

Love your enemies and pray for those who persecute you. (Matthew 5:44)

You cannot serve God and mammon. (Matthew 6:24)

Beware of false prophets, who come to you in sheep's clothing but inwardly are ravenous wolves. You will know them by their fruits. (Matthew 7:15,16)

If any want to become my followers, let them deny themselves and take up the cross and follow me. (Matthew 16:24)

Unless you change and become like little children, you will never enter the kingdom of heaven. (Matthew 18:3)

Let the little children come to me, and do not stop them; for it is to such as these that the kingdom of heaven belongs. (Matthew 19:14)

No one puts new wine in old wineskins; otherwise the wine will burst the skins and the wine is lost, and so are the skins; but one puts new wine into new wineskins. (Mark 2:22)

There is nothing outside a person that by going in can defile, but the things that come out are what defile. (Mark 7:15)

For this reason a man shall leave his father and mother and be joined to his wife, and the two shall become one flesh. So they are no longer two, but one. Therefore what God has joined together, let no one separate. (Mark 10:7–9)

PAUL THE LETTER-WRITER

Paul's letters would have been written down by a scribe or amanuensis, some of whom are named in his letters – Tertius, for instance, who describes himself as 'the writer of this letter' (Romans 16:22). Occasionally Paul would add something in his own hand – 'See what large letters I make when I am writing in my own hand!' (Galatians 6:11). It was obviously important to establish that the letter was genuinely from the apostle himself. The letters were carried by messenger and would have taken days or weeks to arrive. However, the clear intention of Paul was that most of them should be passed on to other churches in the area (see Colossians 4:16 – the letter to the church at Laodicea that he mentions is lost to us).

Several of his letters – especially 1 Corinthians – were clearly written as replies to letters to him from church leaders. It would be fascinating to read what they had said!

The Temple of Hadrian at Ephesus, Turkey. Ephesus was the destination of an important letter of the apostle Paul, and a strategic centre of the church in the days of Paul's missionary activity in Asia Minor (Turkey). It was also probably the home for many years of the apostle John and Mary the mother of Jesus.

*If anyone strikes you on the cheek, offer the other one also;
and from anyone who takes away your coat do not withhold
even your shirt. (Luke 6:29)*

*In my Father's house are many dwelling-places. If it were not
so, would I have told you that I go to prepare a place for you?
(John 14:2)*

*This is eternal life, that they may know you, the only true
God, and Jesus Christ whom you have sent. (John 17:3)*

*For this I was born, and for this I came into the world, to
testify to the truth. Everyone who belongs to the truth listens
to my voice. (John 18:37)*

Wisdom and Wise Sayings   95

The Wisdom of Paul

When the Bible reader reaches the writings of the apostle Paul, found in fourteen letters addressed to churches or individuals – though not all fourteen are undisputedly the work of Paul himself – a completely different literary genre is encountered. These are not chronicles of deeds and events of long ago. They are not poetry or allegory or 'wisdom' (in the Old Testament sense). They are not like the Gospels or the 'Acts of the Apostles', which tell the story of Jesus and of the community which his followers founded. These are *letters* – genuine correspondence, sometimes addressed to an individual (Timothy, for instance) but usually to a church. They were for the most part clearly intended to be read aloud, and they provide a fascinating insight into the personality and beliefs of Paul and also of the life of those early Christian communities.

Letters are Personal

Sadly, in a way, we don't have any of the letters *to* Paul, though it's obvious that sometimes he's replying to specific points they have made or questions they have raised. It's important to remember that these are letters, which need to be read as their original recipients would have read them. They are addressed to specific people in specific places, and deal with specific issues. It's not safe, for that reason, to assume that everything that applies in the church at Corinth in the middle of the first century necessarily applies in the same way to a church in Portsmouth, say, over two thousand years later – or, for that matter, to a quite different church in another part of Greece or Asia Minor in apostolic times. We can see differences between Paul's attitudes to the different churches: some he clearly trusts; some he feels are still immature and need to be strongly led.

The First Christian 'Theologian'

What emerges, in fact, is a picture of Paul as a highly intelligent, well-educated first-century Jew, passionate and at times inclined to be impatient or angry, deeply committed to passing on a faith to which he himself came painfully and traumatically. He has thought through what the implications are of the coming of the Messiah, Jesus, and the meaning of his life and teaching, death and resurrection. He is, if you like, the first Christian 'theologian'.

Consequently, not all that he writes could be called easy going.

Some of it, to be frank, is almost incomprehensibly complicated. But for the most part these letters have a life and vitality – you could say, a 'charm' – which encourages the reader to persist even with the most opaque passages.

Paul was a Jewish scholar who was converted to Christianity on a journey from Jerusalem to Damascus (from which we get our saying, 'Damascus road' experiences). He was carrying authority from the chief priests to find and arrest Christians in the outlying towns. On the way, he and his companions were halted by a bright light. Paul, literally blinded by the light, heard a voice, which identified itself as the voice of Jesus, telling him to stop 'kicking against the goads' – apparently, the religion he was persecuting already had a fascination or attraction for him. He was to proceed into Damascus where a man called Ananias would lay hands on him and restore his sight.

A Powerful Advocate

In the event, Paul was baptized as a Christian in Damascus and almost at once became a powerful advocate for the cause he had previously tried to extinguish. After several years rethinking his philosophy and beliefs he began a new life as a Christian missionary and teacher, being recognized as an apostle of Jesus Christ even though, unlike the other apostles, he had never met Jesus in the flesh.

In the course of this work he founded many small Christian communities and churches, and his letters are mostly written to encourage or instruct them. In the course of doing this we learn quite a lot about Paul himself: a widower, it would seem, who made his living by tent-making but spent most of his time in Christian ministry; a thoughtful, rather analytical teacher; a man who lived by the most rigorous personal standards and expected the same from others. Wrongly, I believe, he is also seen by many modern people as narrow-minded and rather joyless – a misogynist, even – and one who turned the 'straight-forward' teaching of Jesus into a complicated dogmatic system.

In fact, as can be shown from his writings, he was a man who elicited enormous love and affection from others, and expressed it himself. In the context of the first century, far from being a misogynist or a narrow-minded bigot he was liberal and generous hearted. He had a passionate faith in and love for Jesus Christ, and a warmth of affection for those he had come to know in churches all over Asia Minor. For him, in Christ there was neither 'Jew nor Greek, male nor female, slave nor free', but 'all are one' (see Galatians 3:28). Those were revolutionary words for his time!

Slaves and Women

Of course, like most of us, he found it hard to apply his highest ideals to the actual situation in which he found himself. In a society where slavery was the norm, and many argued that the economy would collapse without it, he could see that a Christian slave was his brother while not being able to accord to him the social status that that would seem to demand (you can read him wrestling with this dilemma in his letter to Philemon, written to a Christian slave owner whose slave has run away but subsequently been converted to the faith).

Equally, in a society that accorded women little status beyond decoration and child-bearing, he could assert trenchantly that gender differences were 'nothing' in the sight of God, without always applying the principle in church practice, though it has to be said that women are constantly referred to in his letters as his colleagues and valued partners in ministry – see, especially, the letter to the Philippians.

In all of this he was, I suppose, a man of his time, while at the same time being well ahead of his time! Reading his letters – often very passionate and emotional, sometimes rather academic and closely reasoned – it's possible to get a picture of a real person, hugely gifted, enormously intelligent, almost desperately committed to the task he believed that that vision of Jesus on the road to Damascus had given him. He travelled literally thousands of miles, much of it on foot, across hot and inhospitable territory, to fulfil that vocation. He planted scores of churches and was the main human link between the Jewish world of Jesus and the Gospels and the wider Greco-Roman world of his day. He longed that his fellow-Jews would come to recognize their Messiah, but he also had a driving urge to share what he called the 'incomparable riches of Christ' with the Gentile world.

Did Paul 'Change' the Gospel?

With regard to the notion – widely peddled in some circles – that Paul's gospel was a corruption or distortion, or at any rate an unnecessary elaboration of the 'simple' message of Jesus, there are one or two things to be noted. The first is that the teaching of Jesus wasn't 'simple', even if it was often presented in story and wise sayings. No one who has read the Sermon on the Mount (Matthew 5–7), for instance, could possibly call this 'simple'.

The second point is that two of the Gospel writers, Mark and Luke, were friends and companions of Paul. If he was engaged in a subtle strategy to re-present the message and meaning of Jesus, he obviously hid it very well from them. His letters were written – indeed, his life was probably over, ending with execution in Rome – before the first Gospel, Mark, was written. It is probably more accurate to say that Paul believed and taught exactly the same message as the Gospels, but was applying it to the life of the new church and the lives of new Christians, most of whom had no Jewish background at all. He also gave that message its intellectual undergirding. Standing back a little from the events, he was able to see how the coming of Jesus, and especially his death and resurrection, 'fitted' into the whole scheme of God's salvation. In a book like Romans, for instance, we can see a fine mind grappling with the implications of law and grace – the tension between a loving God who wants to show compassion to failures, and a God of judgment, who expects his creatures to obey his laws. It's not easy reading, but no one who perseveres with it could fail to recognize a brilliant mind and intellect engaged in a vital work of analysis and explanation.

If the message of Jesus in the first century was the most significant new 'idea' to erupt on to the world's stage, then the work and writings of Paul were the principle means by which it reached that world beyond Palestine. Whatever we make of him, and, indeed one could say 'like it or not', Paul is a towering figure in the history of our civilization.

Some Examples of the Wisdom of Paul

Ever since the creation of the world God's eternal power and divine nature, invisible though they are, have been understood and seen through the things he has made. (Romans 1:20.

It is not the hearers of the law who are righteous in God's sight, but the doers of the law who are justified. (Romans 2:13)

Therefore, since we are justified by faith, we have peace with God through our Lord Jesus Christ. (Romans 5:1)

We know that all things work together for good for those who love God, who are called according to his purpose. (Romans 8:28)

I am convinced that neither death, nor life, nor angels, nor rulers, nor things present, nor things to come, nor powers, nor height, nor depth, nor anything else in all creation, will be able to separate us from the love of God in Christ Jesus our Lord. (Romans 8:38–39)

Do not be conformed to this world, but be transformed by the renewing of your minds, so that you may discern what is good and acceptable and perfect. (Romans 12:2)

God's foolishness is wiser than human wisdom, and God's weakness is stronger than human strength. (1 Corinthians 1:25)

Love is patient; love is kind; love is not envious or boastful or arrogant or rude. It does not insist on its own way; it is not irritable or resentful; it does not rejoice in wrong-doing but rejoices in the truth. It bears all things, believes all things, hopes all things, endures all things. Love never ends. (1 Corinthians 13:4–8)

Listen, I will tell you a mystery! We will not all die, but we will all be changed, in the twinkling of an eye, at the last trumpet. (1 Corinthians 15:51–52)

Whatever is true, whatever is honourable, whatever is just, whatever is pure, whatever is pleasing, whatever is commendable, if there is any excellence and if there is anything worthy of praise, think about these things. (Philippians 4:8)

8
The Bible and the Future

To know the future has always been a human ambition, though in fact it's hard to see why any sane person would want to know what's going to happen tomorrow, let alone in ten years' time. As Jesus said, 'Today's troubles are enough for today' (Matthew 6:34).

Despite that, prophets of various shapes and sizes have always had a ready audience, and the Bible has proved a happy hunting ground for those eager to comb its pages for clues about the future. In places, it seems to offer much more than clues. Prophets spoke in plain words and in visions, and their words are recorded. Indeed, there are whole books of the Bible that are largely, if not entirely, prophetic. They don't tell us what has happened, or what is happening now, but what lies ahead. No wonder they have proved fruitful fields for the gatherers of scary warnings and promises of prosperity and bliss.

Prophecy in the Old and New Testaments

To understand the Hebrew prophets it's necessary to understand that the other common title for them was 'seers' – literally, 'people who see'... beyond what the rest of us can see. I find it helpful to think of the revelation of God like an underground river just under the surface of our normal experience. There it flows, a life-giving stream, but ineffective unless somewhere we can gain access to it. In the prophets and seers that stream burst through the surface, like a spring in a desert place, the truth about God bubbling up to the surface and being put into words and visions. So they usually introduced their prophecies with the words, 'Thus says the Lord...'

It's also important to stress that in Hebrew thought 'prophecy' doesn't automatically mean 'foretelling the future', as it does in modern English idiom. It means 'forth-telling' – 'telling forth' the word of God, applying it to specific situations and people. We have already seen the prophet Nathan doing this with King David after the royal act of murder and adultery in the case of Uriah and Bathsheba. Nathan wasn't predicting the future, but explaining from a divine perspective what the consequences of David's behaviour would be. Much biblical prophecy is exactly that – if you (people of Israel, people of Judah) do *this*, the consequence will be *this*.

This is equally true of prophecy in the New Testament. In the early church there were men and women who were recognized as 'prophets'. It seems that their major role was to be open in a more direct way than the rest of the Christians to what God wished to be made known about a particular situation: a warning, perhaps, of consequences, or a promise of help if they followed a certain course. All of this is covered by the idea of 'prophecy'.

However, it's also true that there are large parts of the Bible where the words of prophets and seers are recorded which appear to relate to future events, sometimes to events seen as a long while in the future. You can find this in the later chapters of Daniel, which speak of kingdoms and empires yet to come, and of course in the amazing book of Revelation, with its vision of the ultimate future, of God and Christ (referred to as 'the Lamb') enthroned in heaven.

I say 'appear to relate' because at times there is a suspicion that these visions are using the language and images of foretelling to speak in coded form to people in their own day. Much of Revelation, for instance, can be fairly easily related to the situation of Christians under the early waves of persecution from the Roman emperor – 'Babylon' looks suspiciously like Rome and the emperor like the Antichrist. In that case its message is one of encouragement. Judgment will fall on the apparently invincible persecutor. God's justice will be done and his people will be brought to glory (even if it is the 'glory' of martyrs gathered around the heavenly throne).

Even allowing for that, however, it is clear that the seer of Revelation, who identifies himself as 'John', also offers visions of a more distant future. How should we read these? Are people who pore over them to discover the destiny of the European Community or the timing and location of Armageddon engaged in a fruitful or a fruitless exercise?

Apocalyptic Writing

The problem with Revelation, and also with much of Daniel, and even one part of the Gospels where Jesus talks about the future, is that they are expressed in a style of language with which modern people are almost totally unfamiliar. It's known as 'apocalyptic', and comes from the Greek verb 'to reveal'. These, in other words, are hidden or encoded messages. For various reasons, which we shall consider, they are wrapped up in images, visions or language that needs to be 'uncovered' or decoded.

Sometimes this was done for political reasons, to enable the writer to convey a hidden message to those who were in the know, while it all appeared harmless or meaningless to those 'outside'. Much of the book of Revelation falls into this category. Sometimes it was done to place the onus of interpretation on the reader rather than the writer, rather like Jesus' words at the end of many of his parables, 'He who has ears to hear, let him hear.' As we've already suggested, this places the responsibility on the hearer or reader to use their understanding, insight and faith to unpack its meaning.

We can see a clear example of it in Revelation 13:18, where we are told that the 'number of the beast' – the hideous power that dominates the whole earth – would be 'six hundred and sixty six'. In the world of the Middle East at that time there were no special symbols for numbers – 1, 2, 3 and so on. Instead the letters of the Greek alphabet were used, each letter carrying a numerical equivalence. The letters of the Greek word for 'beast', taken in a mathematical sense, added up to 666. But so, by what the seer regarded as a divine revelation, did the name 'Nero Caesar' when written in Hebrew characters. He was the very emperor who had begun the persecution of Christians. In this coded way Nero could be identified as the evil beast of this vision without the need to set out his name in writing. The device is called *gematria* and was a popular and widely used way of encoding names.

On the other hand, the apocalyptic style of writing could be used to describe visions that the author either did not attempt to interpret, or did not feel able to interpret, leaving that task to the reader (much of the later part of the book of Daniel falls into that category). Yet again, Jesus used this kind of language to prophesy future happenings, not in a detailed or dated sense but in picture language and symbol.

Jewish Tombs on the Mount of Olives in Jerusalem

On the Mount of Olives, facing the Temple Mount in Jerusalem, lie the tombs of many Orthodox Jews. Basing their belief on a literal reading of passages like Daniel chapter 12 and Ezekiel 37:1–14, they await the 'resurrection of the righteous'.

By the time of Jesus belief in resurrection was common among Jews (the Sadducees, who denied the resurrection, were exceptions), but again it was seen as the reviving of earthly bodies rather than the transformation of the whole person which is promised through the resurrection of Jesus (see 1 Corinthians 15:42–55).

An example of the latter is found in a passage from the Gospels often called the 'little apocalypse', in which Jesus responded to a question from his disciples asking when 'all these things' – specifically, the destruction of the Temple – were about to be accomplished (see, for example, Mark 13:3–27). It seems likely that this passage is an edited version of many things that Jesus said on these subjects, perhaps on different occasions, but all brought together here in a single narrative. It includes very specific warnings: 'they will hand you over to synagogues and you will stand before governors and kings because of me', and describes graphically a scene of utter desolation, when 'the inhabitants of Judea' should flee to the mountains for safety. It's probable that these days of suffering and persecution are the ones which followed the Jewish uprising against the Romans in AD 70 and the subsequent devastations wreaked by the empire in revenge. Effectively, that event, which included the destruction of the Temple in Jerusalem, marked the end of the Jewish nation, which was dispersed all over Europe and beyond until the foundation of the modern state of Israel in 1948.

However, in the typical manner of this style of writing, those warnings of an imminent disaster seem to have become confused with other visions of a more distant scene. This is described in Mark 13:24–35, where Jesus is clearly looking on to another time 'after those days, after that suffering', when there will be portents and

The old Jewish cemetery on the Mount of Olives, Jerusalem.

signs in the sky and then 'the Son of Man (the title by which he often referred to himself) would come in clouds with great power and glory'. At that point angelic messengers would 'gather his chosen from the four winds, from the ends of the earth to the ends of heaven'. Here we have what many people would recognize as a prophecy of the 'end of the world' – certainly of the world as we know it.

The Monastery of St John dominates the town of Hora on the Greek island of Patmos. John was in exile on the island when he received the vision that he describes in the book of Revelation.

The disciples had asked 'When will this happen?' – a question people since have often argued about. Jesus, however, was very clear about one thing: no one knows, 'neither the angels in heaven, nor the Son, but only the Father' (Mark 13:32). He was not giving either a blueprint or a timetable for events that lay only in the will of God. Indeed, the very form in which he chose to express himself should have made that clear to them. This is the language of hidden messages, of truths that need to be teased out and comprehended by experience and faith. There *is* a divine purpose, Jesus is saying. The things that will happen do not come about by accident or whim. But we who dwell on earth – and even Jesus while he was 'one of us' – are given only clues and visions and symbols of that distant truth.

That, it seems to me, is the way to read the great apocalypse (that's actually what it's called in Catholic Bibles), the staggering book of Revelation. If you try to read it as a road map or timetable of future events you are sure to get it wrong, mainly because it was never intended to be that. This series of visions that John experienced on the island of Patmos should surely be approached in much the same way as we read modern allegory or even fantasy literature. As soon as you start to say 'What does that mean?' you are losing the plot. Far better to let the images and colours and voices wash over you. As you swim through their deep waters I am sure that you will begin to absorb the

overwhelming 'message' of this extraordinary book, that God is still on the throne of the universe, that evil and cruelty and even natural disasters do not have the last word. That word is always his.

This book spoke with remarkable relevance, for instance, to Christians in China at the time of the revolution under Mao Tse Tung. One who was living there wrote a marvellous and moving commentary on Revelation, calling it *The Lamb upon the Throne*. For them, Babylon was not the ancient Persian city, nor even the imperial Rome which the vision almost certainly identifies, but the new totalitarianism that they felt was about to swamp them and would inevitably lead to great suffering for many Chinese Christians. For them, Revelation was a book whose 'hidden' message became clear through their own experience. Perhaps that is always how it 'works' most effectively.

One thing remains to be said about prophecy in the Bible, and that is that some of it, especially in the writings of the later Hebrew prophets like Isaiah, *is* concerned with foretelling future events and that in some cases we can put those prophecies to the test of time. When we do, we find that they have an uncanny knack of being right!

To take a few examples:

The Birth of Jesus

But you, O Bethlehem of Ephrathah, who are one of the little clans of Judah, from you shall come forth for me one who is to rule in Israel, whose origin is from of old, from ancient days.

THE PROPHET MICAH, EIGHTH CENTURY BC

Joseph also went from the town of Nazareth in Galilee to Judea, to the city of David called Bethlehem, because he was descended from the house and family of David. He went to be registered with Mary, to whom he was engaged and who was expecting a child. While they were there, the time came for her to deliver her child. And she gave birth to her firstborn son (Jesus) and wrapped him in bands of cloth, and laid him in a manger, because there was no place for them in the inn.

LUKE'S GOSPEL, FIRST CENTURY AD, **DESCRIBING THE BIRTH OF JESUS IN AROUND 4** BC

John the Baptist

A voice cries out: 'In the wilderness prepare the way of the Lord, make straight in the desert a highway for our God.'

ISAIAH, SIXTH CENTURY BC

In those days John the Baptist appeared in the wilderness of Judea, proclaiming, 'Repent, for the kingdom of heaven has come near... One who is more powerful than I is coming after me; I am not worthy to carry his sandals.'

MATTHEW'S GOSPEL, FIRST CENTURY AD

The Suffering Saviour

He was despised and rejected by others;
  a man of suffering and acquainted with infirmity;
and as one from whom others hide their faces
  he was despised, and we held him of no account.
Surely he has borne our infirmities
  and carried our diseases;
yet we accounted him stricken,
  struck down by God, and afflicted.
But he was wounded for our transgressions,
  crushed for our iniquities;
upon him was the punishment that made us whole,
  and by his bruises we are healed.
All we like sheep have gone astray;
  we have all turned to our own way,
  and the Lord has laid on him the iniquity of us all.
He was oppressed, and he was afflicted,
  yet he did not open his mouth;
like a lamb that is led to the slaughter,
  and like a sheep that before its shearers is silent,
  so he did not open his mouth.
By a perversion of justice he was taken away.
  Who could have imagined his future?
For he was cut off from the land of the living,
  stricken for the transgression of my people.
They made his grave with the wicked
  and his tomb with the rich,
  although he had done no violence,
  and there was no deceit in his mouth.

ISAIAH, SIXTH CENTURY BC

A reading of the Gospel accounts of the trial, arrest, crucifixion and burial of Jesus reveals remarkable parallels to this passage. He was arrested and stood silent before his accusers. He was beaten and scourged, and then ridiculed both by the soldiers and by the crowds who watched his execution. He had said at supper on the evening of his arrest that his death was 'for the forgiveness of sins' (Matthew 26:28). His trial was certainly a 'perversion of justice', the Roman governor having pronounced that he could 'find no fault in him at all' yet permitted his scourging and crucifixion. He died, and was laid in the tomb of a rich man, Joseph of Arimathea.

The Bible and the Future

The fact that many biblical prophecies like these have been fulfilled has led some people to claim that we can find in the Bible a detailed guide to the future. But even these examples, remarkable as they are, could only have been understood *when they had been fulfilled*. That is a feature of biblical prophecy. It doesn't really exist to give us information about the future, but so that when things happen in its fulfilment we can say, 'That's just what the Bible said.' In other words, biblical prophecy exists to strengthen faith rather than to provide detailed advanced warnings.

Two qualifications ought to be made to that statement, however. The first is that many prophecies in the Bible do no more than set out in effect the inevitable consequences of an action. 'Do this, and this will happen.' In that sense, they are serious warnings about reckless or self-willed behaviour. The prophet is like the parent who says to a child stuffing himself with Easter eggs, 'Eat any more of them and you'll be sick.' Without wishing to be sacrilegious, many of the warnings of the Hebrew prophets sound remarkably like that!

The second qualification is that because God is the lord of history (in the sense that past, present and future are all one to him) his perspective on the passing events of our lives is different from ours. He see the picture whole, as it were. Prophecy is there to remind us that our little stories are simply a part of his greater story. The proper response of the believer to prophecy, then, is probably humility rather than astonishment.

So the different kinds of prophecy in the Bible need to be read in different ways. The warnings of the prophets of Israel and Judah are powerful applications of the principle that actions and choices have consequences. The promises of those same prophets, however, need to be seen in a longer perspective. They tell us, time and again, that God will send an agent of blessing, a deliverer and a saviour to his people, his anointed representative, the Messiah – the word simply means 'anointed one'. We read their promises and we are entitled to ask whether they have now been fulfilled (in the coming of Jesus) or whether, as the Jewish people believe, they still await fulfilment.

The prophetic words of Jesus himself point to a great and terrible 'Day of the Lord', a time of final judgment and justice but also of great hope as he himself returns to earth to bring in what he calls the 'kingdom of God'. Neither of these is a simple concept and both probably involve a great deal of mystery and metaphor, but clearly they point to profound spiritual principles which offer to us both warning and hope.

Finally there are the apocalyptic books and passages, which should probably be read in substantial segments, so as to capture the colour, fantasy and impact of their visions. Surely no one could read of the Four Horsemen of the Apocalypse or the Seven Bowls of the Plagues in Revelation without sensing how vivid and awe-inspiring these chilling visions are. Yet if one reads on, we are drawn into the heavenly city, the New Jerusalem, full of light and beauty, where 'death and mourning and crying and pain will be no more, and where God himself will wipe every tear from their eyes' (Revelation 21:4). Here again, in the most vivid way, is that same paradox of warning and hope, but there is a difference. The threats and the judgment have passed, and now we can move on into the realms of joy and love. Revelation may be a strange book, but the emotions and longings with which it deals are those of every human heart. In an odd way, it makes a wonderful conclusion to the whole Bible!

9
Any Objections?

There are a number of common objections to the Bible, some trivial, others fundamental, which anyone encountering it seriously for the first time would probably raise. They are also the sort of questions which surface from time to time in articles in newspapers and on radio and television programmes. They can't be lightly dismissed by the devout Christian, partly because, as I well know, they can be encountered in most church congregations as well as in the wider public. Here I have tried to deal with them as straight-forwardly as possible, without offering copper-bottomed answers.

Isn't much of the Bible simply a collection of myths and legends, sanctified by the passage of time and its alleged sanctity?

As I've tried to show, the Bible contains a vast variety of material, some of which does have an element of 'myth' (properly understood) and not all of which is, or was meant to be, read as historical or scientific fact. The creation account in Genesis, for instance, is set out in poetic language and can hardly offer an eye-witness' account of events which no human being was there to observe. The extreme ages given for many of the patriarchs in the early part of the Bible are also hardly intended to be read literally. What they emphasize is the contrast between the ancient view of old age (that it was a source of great wisdom and a sign of divine approval) and the modern cult of youth.

On the other hand, much of the Old Testament clearly *does* set out to record actual events, and a good deal of archaeological research has provided surprising evidence of its accuracy. The only real test of a piece of writing is the intention of its author. Was the primary intention to record facts, or to convey a religious or spiritual truth? For the biblical writers the latter intention would almost certainly take precedence over the former.

When we turn to the Gospels we are on firmer ground, if only because we have moved into a more 'modern' view of truth. Luke clearly gives his aim as to present the facts about the life of Jesus, and even if once or twice he seems to get them wrong that doesn't invalidate the intention. Like the others, however, he would surely agree that he was setting out to persuade his readers that Jesus was the Messiah, the Son of God, and the world's Saviour. None of them was a cool, detached 'reporter' of events (if such a person has ever existed!).

In general, the word 'myth' is widely misunderstood in popular modern usage. It does *not* mean 'untrue' but describes a way of conveying truth that goes beyond simple facts. It may involve story, allegory or fantasy, and as I have shown all of those are present in the Bible in some places. The skill is to spot where!

The truth is that the Bible has been subjected to closer and more critical scrutiny over the last two hundred years than any other book in the world. It has withstood that scrutiny remarkably well. The Dead Sea Scrolls, discovered in the 1940s, provided us with much more reliable manuscripts of the Old Testament texts – many hundreds of years older than the ones we had before. If a process of textual corruption had been going on, they should have provided evidence of it. In fact, what they revealed was how accurate the later manuscripts were and how meticulously the scribes had copied them.

Provided we read the Bible intelligently, making due allowance for the different literary forms being used, it could be said to be the most reliable collection of ancient writings history has known, and an unrivalled source of religious wisdom.

The God of the Old Testament seems like a blood-thirsty tyrant, even ordering the slaughter of innocent woman and children.

Yes, at times the picture presented does seem cruel and uncompromising. There's no point in denying that. Indeed, if the only picture we had of God was of the one who commanded the Israelites to slaughter every one of the Amalekites (1 Samuel 15:3), including their women, infants, children and cattle, we would be justified in rejecting it. However, it isn't, and we aren't.

There are several things to bear in mind. Firstly, not to beat about the bush, the Amalekites had 'asked for it' – they had been the implacable enemies of Israel since they first crossed swords, literally, in the desert on the journey from Egypt. That might seem to justify it as a policy for the Israelites but hardly merits divine endorsement.

New Testament manuscripts were generally written on parchment or papyrus in the first centuries of the Christian era, generally in the form of scrolls, and later on parchment bound more or less in book form ('codex'). Because the material was expensive, the writers didn't waste it by putting spaces between words or phrases, which makes reading them a slow and laborious task! In addition there are corrections by scribes and even manuscripts used for a second time, with one text still visible below the other.

Despite all this, thanks to the work of dedicated scholars over several centuries, and the care with which scribes and copyists have done their work, most experts would agree that the New Testament as we find it in our modern Bibles is as near as makes no difference to what the original writers wrote or dictated nearly two thousand years ago.

The earliest surviving fragment of the Gospel of John, dating from AD 125–50.

Secondly, all one can say about such stories in the Old Testament is that the writer *saw* this as an action commanded by God. In Jewish thought, everything that happened was part of the divine will – nothing happened anywhere independently of the purpose of God. In that case, the slaughter was in some way part of the divine order of things. At the time, and to that chronicler, God did it – just as, to put the balance right, the Jews were given over to slavery or exile by the same purpose of God.

The important thing here is the principle of *progressive revelation*. The Bible is a saga, not a series of isolated incidents. As the revelation of God progresses through its pages we see emerging a clearer and clearer picture of what he is like, for all the world like adjusting the focus through a telescope. So the simple picture of a

God who 'walked in the garden in the cool of evening' in the third chapter of Genesis developed into the image of the tribal God of Israel – greater than the other gods, but almost to be regarded as one of them (see, for instance, 2 Chronicles 2:5: 'our God is greater than other gods'). From that we have the slow unfolding of the full revelation of *Yahweh*, 'I AM', the one, eternal, personal God of the whole earth. It's not that he is greater than the 'other gods'; they aren't gods at all. There is only one, and that is *Yahweh*.

We then find the psalmist at times singing of a God of infinite loving-kindness and the late, great Hebrew prophets speaking of a God who nurses his people like a mother or cares for them like a shepherd cares for his lambs. Again, that prepares the reader for the further understanding of God which Jesus brought us: a God of forgiveness, mercy and above all love – still utterly opposed to evil and injustice, but totally on the side of the weak and powerless and whose concern reaches out far beyond Israel to people of every race and language.

To pick on one part of that unfolding revelation as though it were the whole thing is to shut the book before you have found out where the story is going – and then complaining that it's incomplete!

It's all like Chinese whispers. The stories of miracles and so on simply grew and grew as they were passed on.

This is commonly believed but in the case of the Gospels (to which it is usually applied) quite wrong-headed. The earliest account of something Jesus said is in the apostle Paul's first letter to the Corinthians, written around AD 54, just over twenty years after the crucifixion – not very long for those 'Chinese whispers' to work. The first Gospel is generally reckoned to be Mark's, probably written ten to fifteen years after that. There would still have been plenty of people alive, including most of the apostles, to have contradicted exaggerations or errors of fact. In fact, Paul uses exactly that argument later in that same letter to the Corinthians, where he claims that over 500 people saw the risen Jesus, 'most of whom are still alive' (15:6).

Another factor is relevant, the ability of people in the pre-literacy age to remember accurately. There has been much evidence of this from tribal myths in Africa and elsewhere, passed on for centuries by word of mouth and yet remarkably preserved. Often the key to this is the degree of importance attached to the 'message' – the more important, the more accurately it is remembered. We can imagine that the first Christians were desperately anxious to remember accurately the teaching and activities of Jesus. As they were told them by the first witnesses, they were cherished, memorized and passed on. This 'oral tradition' probably lies behind much of the material in the Gospels, certainly those of Matthew, Mark and Luke. It may help to account for the fact that Gospels compiled at different places in the Roman world – Ephesus, Rome, Jerusalem perhaps – should be so similar, indeed identical in many places. I am sure that we can hear the authentic voice of Jesus the Teacher in those first three Gospels – John, probably writing some time after the others, has a different purpose: to offer a reflection of the enormous impact the life and teaching of Jesus made on his contemporaries.

I don't believe in miracles at all. Surely that makes the Bible a closed book to me?

Well, yes, there are a lot of 'miracles' in the Bible, some in the Hebrew Scriptures but even more in the Gospels. To remove that element from it altogether would emasculate it. And for Christians, for whom the centre point of their faith is a miracle – the resurrection of Jesus – it would render their faith 'futile', as Paul put it (1 Corinthians 14:14). However, it is necessary to distinguish between two rather different things, both often referred to as 'miracles' in our English versions of the Bible. The first is an event so staggering that it falls outside the realm of rational explanation (even though it may, on investigation, have a reasonable cause). I think of the Israelites crossing the Red Sea led by Moses, an event always seen as a miracle by Jewish people, yet explained quite rationally in the text of the book of Exodus: 'The Lord drove the sea back by a strong east wind all night and turned the sea into a dry land' (Exodus 14:21). Many, though admittedly not all, of the Old Testament miracles fall into this category.

The second is a divine 'sign', which is how John's Gospel refers to the miracles of Jesus. They were not simply staggering and amazing, but *evidences* of the power and involvement of God. They did not happen in order to impress the onlookers, but to demonstrate that Jesus was the Son of God. Unless one is prepared to argue that nothing ever or anywhere has happened that goes beyond the boundaries of our present human knowledge and understanding (which makes the creation itself or the existence of consciousness look suspect), surely we might expect it to happen when the Son of God was on earth?

THE BIBLE ALONGSIDE OTHER SCRIPTURES

The Bible (the Hebrew and Christian Scriptures) embraces a much longer history in its compilation than the other world scriptures. It's impossible to be precise, but elements of the Old Testament were clearly in written form over a thousand years before Christ. There was extensive editorial work done on ancient texts in the sixth century BC, when most of the Hebrew canon (list of authorized books) was settled, though the process was not complete until the first century BC. The New Testament was almost all written before the end of the first century AD, but the Christian canon was not finally agreed until early in the fifth century AD.

I'm only interested in the Bible as a literary masterpiece. Surely that's its only real value to us today?

By all means enjoy the Bible as a literary masterpiece! However, when you describe it as that, I suspect that you are referring not to the Bible as it was originally written, but to the King James ('Authorized') Version of the Bible in English. That was, indeed, a masterpiece, translating the Hebrew and Greek biblical texts into the matchless English of Shakespeare's time. The difficulty is that while some of the Bible in its original texts is of great literary value – I'm thinking of Hebrew poetry in the Psalms and the Song of Solomon, for instance – most of it is less concerned with literary merit than with either recording the unfolding story of the people of Israel or conveying deep truths about a revelation of God. Certainly there is not much 'literary merit' in the Gospels of Mark, Matthew and Luke, or in the letters of Paul, at any rate in terms of the actual language they used. There are exceptions, and I think we can catch from time to time in the Gospels the authentic voice of Jesus the preacher, which is brilliantly persuasive. And once or twice, in a moment of passion, Paul is moved to real eloquence. Luke writes good Greek, and there is what we might call 'literary merit' in his skill as a storyteller. Indeed, all of the writers of the Gospel show many literary skills in the arrangement and presentation of the story of Jesus, but their actual language is often a good deal less than elegant.

I suppose what I am saying is that it's fine to read the Bible as 'literature', but that to read it solely with that objective would be to miss the wood for the trees. Its writers were not concerned to be literary giants, but to point us to an understanding of the ways of God. If we were to miss that, we would miss the whole point of the exercise.

Why the Bible – why not some other 'holy book', or the teachings of my favourite guru or current spiritual hero?

In one sense this can only be answered with a 'faith claim' – that the Bible is unique because it is uniquely inspired by God, but of course that won't do if you don't believe it! So let's try to apply some reasoning to the question.

Perhaps we could start with the existence of God (if we can't agree about that, there's no point in the discussion about whether this particular book is a unique revelation of his truth). If God exists, then by definition he is eternal, all-powerful and all-knowing. Not much point in a god who isn't. But if he is, then in those respects he is utterly unlike us. We are mortal, very limited in our power and partial in our knowledge.

It seems to follow that if we are to know the truth about God he must tell it to us, because if we could work it out for ourselves we'd be all-knowing, like him. From that one premise we can base the idea of the self-revelation of God. If we are to know anything about him, he must reveal it to us.

Obviously that revelation would need to be in terms which human beings can understand – to put it another way, it must be within the limits of our own experience. All through human history, people have recorded their own feelings and experiences of the 'divine', and that is, of course, part of the 'evidence' about God. So all the 'holy writings', in which wise and holy people have passed on their experiences of God, are valuable contributions to our understanding of him. Much of the Old Testament is taken up with one nation's experience of God, as the people of Israel and their prophets struggled to understand his ways with them.

To understand fully, however, or as fully as we humanly can, it must surely be necessary for God himself to reveal the truth to the human race. That is what Christians believe happened in the life and teaching of Jesus. In him, they believe, God was as fully present in a human life as he could possibly be. To see him (as he claimed – John 14:9) is to 'see the Father'. Now that is, of course, a statement of faith, but all the evidence that we have suggests that Jesus reflects all the best that we can imagine, in moral purity, in love and acceptance, in wisdom and generosity of spirit. This must be what God is like!

Jesus accepted the Hebrew Scriptures. They were his Bible. He had not come to contradict them, but to 'fulfil' them, he said. The picture of God that they gave, with increasing clarity as the revelation progressed, was consistent with the heavenly Father that he came to reveal. For me, the fact that Jesus respected the 'Old Testament' is the best reason for respecting it myself. He also assured his apostles that the Holy Spirit would 'teach them everything, and remind them of all that he had said to them' (John 14:26). That is why I also respect the writings of the New Testament.

I agree that that's a circular argument, but it provides a rational basis for my belief that the Bible is unique in its revelation of God. Yes, there may be – I'm sure there are – valuable insights into the divine in other scriptures and through other sources, but for me and for millions of others the Bible is in a unique way the 'Word of God'. Perhaps the only way truly to test that for yourself is to read it, which, after all, is what this present book is all about.

MIDDLE EASTERN GODS

The Jews were scathing about the gods of the 'heathen', which the Hebrew prophets derided as fit only to be chopped up and used as firewood (see Isaiah 44:15 for a hilarious picture of a man chopping down a tree and using some of it to make a fire and bake bread, and the rest of it to create his god). However, on one notable occasion the Israelites themselves fell into the same trap. While Moses was away up the mountain of Sinai communing with God, the people made themselves a gold bull-calf, worshipped it and said, 'These are your gods, O Israel, who brought you up out of the land of Egypt' (Exodus 32:4).

This clay figurine, dating from the tenth to the seventh centuries BC, was probably worshipped as a household deity. It depicts Asherah or Ashtoreth, the Canaanite goddess of fertility and consort of the principal god, El (known in the Bible as Baal).

10
The Reduced Bible

Any reader might be daunted by the prospect of tackling the entire Bible and as I have already suggested anyone who set off hopefully from the opening chapter of Genesis would do well to reach the end of that book with their enthusiasm intact, let alone the end of the whole Bible. I suppose it's much the same for anyone tackling the entire works of Shakespeare, which may be why the Reduced Shakespeare Company offers highly abbreviated versions of all the plays rolled into one – all the story but none of the frills!

In this final section of the book I'm offering the reader a similar approach to the Bible. The only difference is that you have to do the actual reading, but by the generous provision of a kind of filleting job on the text you can cover all the essential parts of the 'plot' and have tasters of all the main elements in the Bible without having to wade through its 1,200 or so pages. It takes the Bible in its traditional order, which of course is not the order in which the books were necessarily written, and each section has a brief summary of its contents, rather like the synopsis that the programme of an opera in Italian offers the audience.

If you would like to undertake a 'skim read' of the whole Bible, then this is probably the easiest way to do it – but it's important that you pursue the reading from beginning to end and don't give in to the temptation to dip in here and there or pick and mix. Many of the problems people have with the Bible flow from precisely that approach. Although, as we've seen, it has many authors and is a compilation of writings from a period of about a thousand years, the Bible really does have a unity. At least this skimmed version retains something of that.

Each book of the Bible is listed, and then the passages suggested for reading follow, together with a brief resume of what you can expect to find in them. Those starred are considered essential – the difference, I suppose, between semi-skimmed and skimmed!

The Old Testament

Genesis

The name means 'Beginning' – deals with origins: the origins of the earth, of plant, animal and human life; and the origins of the people through whom the Lord would one day bless 'every nation'. These would be the descendants of Abraham. It is clearly a compilation from various ancient stories and chronicles, brought together to show how the purpose of God was slowly being worked out right from the beginning. Compared with other books, I suggest a rather substantial amount of Genesis should be read, because it lays the foundations of much of what is to follow.

To read

Chapters 1–3: The story of the creation – first of the earth, its plants, animals, birds and people, followed by the story of the creation of the sexes to complement each other. Chapter 3 is the story of the temptation of Eve and Adam, and of its dire consequences.

Chapters 6–8: The story of the flood. It begins with some unspecified corruption of the human species (inter-marriage with non-humans?) and God's decision to wipe it out and start again. Then God decides to spare righteous Noah and his family, who are told to build the ark, in which they and the animals can survive the flood which wiped out everything else. The story ends with a promise from God that he will never do anything like that again.

Chapter 12:1–8: The call of Abram to leave his home in Ur and journey westwards to a land which he would be shown, which the Lord would give to his descendants for ever. Abram calls on the 'name of the Lord'.

Chapter 17: Abram ('ancestor') is renamed 'Abraham' ('ancestor of a multitude'). God promises him that he will be the founder of a great nation, which will inhabit the land of Canaan, and as a sign of this 'covenant' requires all of Abraham's male offspring to be circumcised. Sarai is renamed 'Sarah' and promised a son, to be called Isaac, who would inherit this covenant agreement.

Chapter 27:1–29: Isaac, now an old man, is tricked into giving his blessing to his younger son Jacob, who thus inherits the promises.

Chapter 30:1–23: Jacob is married twice, to Leah, who bears him ten sons, and to his favoured wife Rachel, who bears him two, Joseph and Benjamin. These twelve are the founding fathers of the twelve tribes of Israel.

Chapters 37–47: (This is a long passage, but it covers a vital part of the story, without which much of the Old Testament makes no sense!) Here is recounted the fascinating story of Joseph being sold by his brothers as a slave and ending up in the court of the pharaoh, king of Egypt. His wisdom saves the country from the effects of a devastating famine and he becomes second only to Pharaoh in status. Eventually his brothers and their families and his elderly father Jacob join him in Egypt, where they settle in land provided for them by the king, in Goshen. Here they prosper, though Jacob dies there.

Exodus

As you might guess from its title, this is the story of the 'exodus' or departure of the Israelites (Hebrews) from Egypt, led by Moses. It includes the seminal story of the giving of the Law of God at Sinai.

To read

Chapters 1–2: Things go wrong in Egypt! Many years have passed, the Hebrews (the descendants of Jacob) have multiplied and a new pharaoh regards them as a threat. Jewish baby boys are to be killed at birth. However, young baby Moses survives through a stratagem of his mother and is adopted by Pharaoh's daughter, though continuing to be cared for by his own mother. Eventually, having killed an

Egyptian slave-master, the young man Moses flees Egypt and finds refuge in the land of Midian. He marries Zipporah, the daughter of a Midianite priest, and settles there.

Chapters 3–4: The great turning point in the history of the Israelites – Moses at the burning bush. God calls him to return to Egypt and with divine backing ensure the release of the Hebrews from slavery. Despite many (sometimes amusing) objections by Moses, he reluctantly accepts the task.

Chapters 5–12: (Again, a long passage, but vital to the whole story – also worth reading for its own sake!): The plagues of Egypt, the Passover and the eventual exodus of the Israelites from Egypt. Moses tells them their destination: a promised land 'flowing with milk and honey'.

Chapter 12: The 'Passover'.

Chapter 14: Crossing the Red (or Reed) Sea – one of the great stories of human history. The Israelites begin their long journey which, though they didn't know it then, would take them forty years in all.

Chapter 16: The gift of 'food from heaven', manna.

Chapter 20: Sinai, and the giving of the Law. The 'Ten Commandments' are handed over to Moses, 'written on tablets of stone'.

Chapter 32: The Golden Calf. While Moses is a long time up Mount Sinai the people persuade his brother Aaron to make them a 'god' which they can see and worship. When Moses discovers what he has done he is distraught at their idolatry. The people are punished.

Most of the later part of Exodus is taken up with detailed instructions for the building, equipping and decoration of the Tabernacle, the tent in which the 'ark of the covenant' was kept throughout their journey. The ark contained the Law, some manna, Moses' staff and Aaron's rod, and became the symbol to the Jews of the presence of God in their midst. There is no need to include this in our Reduced Bible.

Leviticus

This book is a detailed manual of ritual, social and religious law for the people of Israel. The only part which is relevant to our Reduced Bible is the description of the Day of Atonement, still observed (though without animal sacrifices) by the Jewish people each Autumn. It is an observation in which repentance for sins and prayers for forgiveness are made by the whole people, for the whole nation. This is found in chapter 16.

Numbers

The book of Numbers, as its name implies, spends a lot of time setting out the size and details of the various tribes as they resume their journey from Sinai towards the promised land. However, more or less from chapter 10 it does pick up that story – it's been a long parenthesis from Exodus chapter 32! – and the second stage of the exodus gets under way.

To read
Chapters 13–14:25: The account of the spies who were sent to report back on the defences and tribes of the land of Canaan, the 'promised land'. The spies brought back a negative report: the land is indeed fertile but its inhabitants are fierce and warlike, to the extent that the Israelites could not hope to defeat them. However, one spy, Caleb, together with a colleague, Joshua, presented a minority report, claiming that they would be 'well able to overcome it'. The people were swayed by the majority view, of course, and the suggestion was made that they should find another leader and go back to Egypt. The Lord was so angry at this that he vowed that none of the people who had seen his signs and glory on the journey from Egypt would see the promised land. The only exceptions would be Caleb and Joshua.

Chapter 20: Moses loses his patience and goes beyond God's instructions when bringing the people water from a rock at Meribah. The Lord was so displeased that he told Moses that he, too, would never actually enter the promised land. The people set out towards Canaan. Aaron dies on Mount Hor and Eleazar is made high priest in his place.

Deuteronomy

This book repeats much detail from Exodus and Numbers, but does advance the story of the journey to the promised land as well. Much of the book, however, is occupied with setting out details of the laws and rituals of the emerging people, including repetition of the Ten Commandments. Some of these laws – for example, the rules of warfare in chapter 20 – are interesting, but in terms of the story of the people of Israel we can move on to the last few chapters.

To read

Chapter 31: Moses 'retires' at an advanced age and appoints Joshua as his successor. Having 'written the words of the Law in a

MOSES

The first five books of the Bible (in Greek, Pentateuch) are also called 'The Books of Moses', but on every ground it must be unlikely that he actually wrote all, or possibly any of them. They are the books of Moses because they make up the body of the Torah, the Teaching or Law of Israel. Exodus, Deuteronomy and Numbers also give us the story of Moses, of course, from his birth and escape from execution to his death on Mount Nebo. As usual, they are capped with his 'last thoughts' and commandments, and also the account of his death and a final epitaph ('he knew the Lord face to face') – which he could hardly have written himself!

The books of Moses occupy over a quarter of the Hebrew Scriptures and about 17 per cent of the whole Bible.

book' (verse 24) Moses ordered that it should be placed in the ark of the covenant as a permanent reminder to the people.

Chapter 34: The death of Moses – the Lord having 'showed him' from the peak of Mount Pisgah the promised land stretched out before him. The chapter ends with a moving tribute to the man who had led the Israelites for so long, and through such apparently impossible obstacles, to the borders of Canaan, which lay across the River Jordan below him.

Joshua
To read
Chapters 1–2: Joshua prepares the people to cross the River Jordan and take possession of the land that the Lord had promised them. Spies are sent into Jericho, the fortified city which barred their way. The prostitute Rahab helped them.

Chapters 3–4: Crossing Jordan – the second 'dry land' crossing of their long journey. The ark of the Lord as the 'bridge'.

Chapter 5:13–6: The fall of Jericho – 'the walls came tumbling down'. Its divinely ordered destruction.

Adoration of the Golden Calf from the Bible Mozarabe, Spanish School, tenth century.

Chapter 24: Joshua renews the 'covenant' and the people pledge to serve the Lord only. The death of Joshua and the burial of Joseph's bones.

Judges (the rulers of Israel after Joshua)
To read

Chapters 6–7:21: The story of Gideon and the defeat of the Midianites.

Chapters 13–16 (optional but interesting!): The story of Samson – his birth, marriage to Delilah, a Philistine, her deceit and his death in the temple of Dagon.

Ruth
The story of the young alien woman who married an Israelite and became a distant ancestor of Jesus.

To read

Chapter 1:16,17: Ruth's memorable pledge to remain with her Jewish mother-in-law.

1 Samuel
To read

Chapter 1: The birth of Samuel – his mother offers him to the Lord's service.

Chapter 3: The Lord calls the boy Samuel. He becomes the prophet of the Lord.

Chapters 8–10:1: The Israelites ask for a king and are given Saul.

Chapter 16: The Lord rejects Saul as king and tells Samuel to find a new one – David, the shepherd boy.

Chapter 17:1–51: David and Goliath.

2 Samuel
To read

Chapter 1: The death of Saul and his son Jonathan. David's lament over them.

Chapter 5: David becomes king of the united kingdom of Israel and Judah and drives the Jebusites out of Jerusalem.

Chapters 11–12: David and Bathsheba – adultery, murder and punishment.

1 Kings
To read

Chapter 1:27–31: David confirms that his son Solomon will be the next king.

Chapter 3: Solomon asks God for the gift of wisdom.

Chapter 8: The new Temple built by Solomon is dedicated and the ark of the Lord installed there.

The rest of 1 Kings is an account of the various kings who followed Solomon, most of whom failed to please the Lord. Parallel to this are the deeds of the great prophets Elijah and his successor Elisha.

David with the Head of Goliath by Michelangelo Merisi da Caravaggio (1571–1610).

To read

Chapter 18:16–end: Elijah confronts the prophets of Baal on Mount Carmel.

2 Kings

To read

Chapter 2: Elijah is caught up into heaven. Elisha is appointed prophet in his place.

Chapter 5: (optional, but interesting): The healing of Naaman, the leper.

The remaining chapters up to chapter 17 give a catalogue of the kings of Israel and Judah, now separate kingdoms.

Chapter 17:1–23: The Assyrians conquer Israel (the northern kingdom) and take the people into captivity.

Chapter 18:1–8: Hezekiah, the good king of Judah (the southern kingdom).

Chapter 19:14–17; and 35–37: The Assyrians are defeated after Hezekiah prays to the Lord for deliverance.

Chapter 24:18–25: King Zedekiah 'did evil' and the Lord delivered him into the hands of Nebuchadnezzar, king of Babylon. Jerusalem is conquered and the people of Judah are taken into captivity.

1 Chronicles

This book covers ground already recorded in 2 Samuel and 1 Kings, though from a 'priestly' rather than 'palace' perspective. For the purpose of a Reduced Bible it can probably be omitted.

2 Chronicles

Again, this book covers much the same period of history as the books of Kings.

To read

Chapters 30–31:1: Hezekiah restores the Passover, to the people's great joy.

Chapter 34: The young King Josiah, who came to the throne aged eight, similarly restored true worship after a period of apostasy, and also rediscovered the Law of the Lord.

Ezra

This book, and that of Nehemiah, deal with events in the fifth century BC when the Jews were given permission by the king of Persia to rebuild the Temple in Jerusalem. Ezra seems to have held some official position in the royal court, though he was a Jew.

To read

Chapter 1:1–7: Cyrus the king gives permission and the people respond.

Chapter 6:13–22: Despite opposition and ridicule, the people continue to build under the leadership of the prophet Haggai and also Nehemiah (see below). Finally the Temple was dedicated and the former exiles celebrated the Passover.

Chapter 7:5–10; 27–28: Ezra returns to Jerusalem with fresh authority from Artaxerxes, the new king, and accompanied by leading men from among the Israelites.

Nehemiah

This book recounts the same events as Ezra but from the perspective of Nehemiah, who actually supervised the work.

To read

*Chapter 8: Once the wall of the city was built and people had returned to settle in Jerusalem, Ezra read the Law of Moses aloud to the crowd in the city square. In celebration the people built booths on their roofs – the origin of the Jewish Feast of Tabernacles.

Esther

The only book in the Bible that never mentions God! It relates the courage of a Jewish woman, Esther, who became one of the wives of King Xerxes during a time of captivity and exile. It's a story well worth reading, very much part of Jewish history, but not essential to a Reduced Bible.

Job

The book begins with the story of a

rich man, Job, who loses everything – family, home, cattle, riches. Yet he does not curse God. This calamity is presented in the story as a result of a challenge between Satan and God – would this godly man curse God if he lost all his possessions? The story is of very ancient and probably pre-Israelite origin.

Most of the rest of the book is taken up with long discourses of advice from Job's three friends, Eliphaz, Bildad and Zophar. They offer various approaches to the problem of undeserved suffering, but the book's eventual answer comes from the Lord himself.

To read

Chapter 38: In a striking example of Hebrew poetry at its most eloquent, the Lord answers Job.

Chapter 42:1–6: Job's humble response to God.

Chapter 42:7–end: The story has a happy ending!

Psalms
The prayer book and the hymn book of Israel. For purposes of a Reduced Bible I suggest two of the best known and most memorable psalms from the collection.

To read

Psalm 23: The 'Shepherd Psalm'.

Psalm 139:1–18: The constant presence of God.

Proverbs
A book of 'wise sayings' ostensibly by Solomon, the wise king of Israel. A selection of these sayings was given in the chapter on Wisdom Literature. For the purpose of a Reduced Bible it can probably be omitted.

Ecclesiastes
Another 'Wisdom' book – sermons from a wise if slightly world-weary preacher!

To read

Chapter 3:1–15: A beautiful poem on 'time'.

Chapter 12:1–7: Old age, decline and death – as a warning to youth!

The Song of Solomon
The only truly erotic book in the Bible, ascribed to Solomon, who should have known all about it having had seven hundred wives and three hundred concubines. It is an eloquent celebration of erotic love, told in the form of a dialogue poem between two lovers, presumably bride and bridegroom. Those who think that the Bible is puritanical should probably read it through; others may omit it as surplus to the requirements of a Reduced Bible – but you may regret it!

THE PSALMISTS

The book of Psalms – the hymn-book of Israel – is a compilation of 150 songs of praise, repentance, prayer, longing and searching for or questioning God. Some were obviously more appropriate for public worship – the Songs of Ascent, for instance (120–134). Others are intensely personal (51, 42), or angry (22, 109), or full of sadness and regret (137). It could be said of the Psalms that 'all human life is here'.

They are traditionally described as the Psalms of David, but it is unlikely that he wrote all of them – he never went into exile, for instance (Psalm 137). In any case, the style of the poetry varies, in the way it does with poets in other cultures. Nevertheless, King David had a reputation as a musician and singer (see, for instance, 1 Samuel 18:10), and there is no good reason why he should not have been both the author of many of the psalms and also a patron of other psalmists.

Sometimes there are musical directions given with the text of the psalm – the tune to which it is to be sung, or an appropriate point for some special cadenza or stroke of percussion, possibly ('Selah' can be found in several psalms, perhaps indicating the latter, and other musical directions can be found in the headings of the psalms – see nos. 76, 77 or 80, for instance).

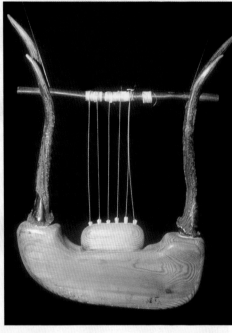

A reconstruction of a form of lyre known as a nevel, Haifa Music Museum.

To read

Chapter 2:10–12: – 'Arise, my love, my fair one, and come away; for now the winter is past, the rain is over and gone. The flowers appear on the earth; and the time of singing has come...'

Chapter 4:16: An invitation to the bridegroom to 'come to his garden and eat its choicest fruits'.

Isaiah

We now come to the great Hebrew prophets, who take the revelation of God on to another level. 'Isaiah' is the name of the whole book, but it is generally agreed that it records the sayings of at least two prophets, one of whom prophesied in the seventh century BC before Jerusalem fell to Sennacherib, and the second ('Deutero-Isaiah', or Second Isaiah) in the sixth century BC from the days when the captivity came to an end. The message of the first is of inevitable judgment if the people did not repent of their sins. The message of the second is of hope for the future, both in the restoration of Jerusalem but also in the greater fulfilment of God's purposes for the whole world.

To read

*Chapter 1:1–20: The heart of Isaiah's message in twenty verses – stay as you are, and disaster; turn to the Lord, and eat the good of the land.

Chapter 6: The prophet's dramatic calling and the commission God gave him.

Chapter 9: A glimpse of the more hopeful future – a child would be born, light would dawn, endless peace would follow.

*Chapter 11:1–10: A famous passage, often read in the Service of Seven Lessons and Carols at Christmas, and seen by Christians as a prophecy of the descendant of David, Jesus, who would one day bring in a new reign of peace and justice.

Chapters 13–26: Judgment on the surrounding nations, culminating in the judgment of the people of Judah, confident and secure in their great city of Jerusalem. (There is no need to read all of these, once you have got a flavour of them!)

*Chapter 35: A sudden parenthesis of hope – a glimpse of the future when the wilderness will be glad and the desert blossom. Here the prophecy turns to poetry.

Chapter 39: The final judgment – Isaiah warns king Hezekiah that all the riches of the court will one day be carried off to Babylon, though the king consoles himself that it will all happen after his days are over.

Second Isaiah (chapter 40 on)

Chapter 40:1–11: The promise of comfort, forgiveness and restoration... and the 'coming' of God himself to save and 'tenderly care' for them.

Chapter 42:1–4: Often taken as another prophecy of the promised Messiah, though in fact the New Testament applies the words in v3 ('a bruised reed... a smouldering wick') to John the Baptist rather than Jesus (Matthew 12:20).

Chapter 52:7–10: Good news for God's people and a revelation for 'all nations'.

Chapter 53: The 'suffering servant' of the Lord – a passage which Christians have always seen as a clear prophecy of the suffering and death of Jesus 'for our iniquities'.

Chapter 55: A beautiful and poetic invitation to the spiritually hungry and thirsty to 'come and drink' – no cost, no payment, simply 'grace' (unearned favour). Also a call to 'seek the Lord while he may be found'.

Chapter 60:1–3: The glory of the Lord will draw nations and kings to the light. This element in second Isaiah begins to emphasize the ancient promise that the call of Abraham would be for the blessing of the whole world, not just the Jewish people.

Fresco of *Ezekiel and Jeremiah* by the School of Avignon. From the Palace of the Popes at Avignon.

Chapter 61:1–3: The passage Jesus read in the synagogue at Nazareth (Luke 4:16–21). He also rather daringly claimed that it was being 'fulfilled' that very day.

Chapter 65:17–25: A famous picture of the 'golden age' of blessing to be brought in by the coming of the promised Messiah. The book of Revelation draws on these ideas in its picture of the heavenly 'Jerusalem' (21:1–4).

Jeremiah

The prophet Jeremiah is usually regarded as a prophet of doom – in fact, his name has become a by-word for misery! He prophesied during the final years of the kingdom of Judah before its conquest by Nebuchadnezzar, king of Babylon, and the carrying off of its leading citizens, including King Zedekiah, into captivity – so perhaps it's not surprising that its dominant note is doom! On the other hand, as we shall see, and like all the great Hebrew prophets, there are also several passages looking on to a new age, a time of restoration and renewal.

To read

Chapter 1: Jeremiah's call by God and a summary of the message he was to preach –

that the disaster which was imminent and would come from the north was a judgment on the people of Judah for their idolatry and sins.

Chapter 4:1–4: What the people of Israel and Judah would need to do to avoid the judgment of God.

Chapter 11:1–13: The heart of the people's sin was that they had wilfully broken their covenant relationship with the Lord.

*Chapter 18:1–10: The metaphor of the potter and the clay is used to represent God's involvement in human destiny. This image is picked up by the apostle Paul in the New Testament (Romans 9:19–21).

Chapter 23:1–8: A promise that God will one day bring his banished people back to their promised land. Some have seen this as a prophecy of the return of the Jewish 'dispersion' to Israel in modern time.

Chapter 30:1–22: A typically paradoxical passage, on the one hand promising that God would break 'the yoke of slavery on their necks' (v8) and restore them to their promised land, and on the other assuring them that despite this they would not go unpunished (v11) – indeed, their wound was 'incurable' (v12). However, those who had plundered them would be plundered (v16). Then, with a sharp shift of mood, we are into a picture of merry-making as the city of Jerusalem is being rebuilt on its ancient mound (vv18,19). Don't expect consistency in a vision!

The rest of the book carries us remorselessly through to the eventual sacking of Jerusalem and the carrying off of its king and leading people into captivity. The final punishment by the Lord of their conquerors, the Babylonians, is recounted at some length, but Jeremiah's worst anger seems to be reserved for the kings of Judah who ignored his warnings, and especially King Jehoiakim, who cut up and burnt a scroll bearing his message (36:9–32). However, there is a final note of hope (52:31–end) – a new king of Babylon acts kindly to the captive king of Judah.

Lamentations

The title tells you almost everything about this Hebrew poem of lament over the captivity. In terms of a Reduced Bible there is no need to read it, unless you would like to sample a particularly fine example of Hebrew poetry, which is not based on rhyme or metre but on the balancing of ideas. It's called 'parallelism' and this poem is full of splendid examples:

*The joy of our hearts
has ceased;
Our dancing has been
turned to mourning.*
LAMENTATIONS 5:15

Ezekiel

Ezekiel, the third of the great Hebrew prophets, began his ministry in the fifth year of the exile which Jeremiah described in his closing chapter – indeed, his call from God came as he was 'among the exiles by the River Chebar' (1:1). It is not an easy book to read, even for established students of the Bible, but there are passages in it which are relevant to the overall themes of the Scriptures and a number of visions of extraordinary power and imagination. The first of these is in chapter 1.

To read

Chapter 1:4–end: I once asked a primary school class to try to draw this vision and the results were, to say the least, mind-blowing! Perhaps it needs the visual imagination of a child to appreciate it. Certainly the imagery is powerful – a vast engine with wheels and eyes, which can move in every direction, up as well as down, driven by the 'spirit' within it. Above this vehicle is a splendid figure, 'something that seemed like a human form'. In the end, the prophet is reduced to an everyday metaphor: 'Like the bow in a cloud on a rainy day, such was the appearance of the splendour' (v28).

Chapter 2: From this vision a voice spoke to Ezekiel calling him to be his messenger to the 'rebellious people' of Israel and Judah.

Chapter 3:14–21: The reluctant prophet is lifted by the 'spirit' and set down among the exiles. He sat among them, sharing their misery – and then received his divine commission. He must speak whatever God tells him to speak, without fear or favour. Otherwise he, not the people, would be held responsible for their sins.

*Chapter 13:8–16: The perils of false prophecy – those who cry 'Peace!' where there is no peace (v10). Jesus had something to say on this, too (Matthew 7:15–19).

Chapters 4–41: The judgments of God on all the powers and nations and tribes of the ancient world, especially the most powerful, Babylon and Egypt, and also on Israel and Judah. They are not required reading for the Reduced Bible, apart from the passages noted below.

*Chapter 36:24–32: The promise of a renewed Israel, with a 'new heart', cleansed from the past and living under God's blessing.

*Chapter 37:1–14: The vision of the valley of dry bones. Like all

the other prophets, Ezekiel occasionally pauses in denunciation to offer a vision of hope in the future. This vivid picture is of dry bones being re-animated by the Spirit of God – 'these bones are the whole house of Israel' (v11). The spiritual song from the days of slavery in America picked up these images of hope ('Dem bones, dem bones, dem dry bones... Now hear de word of de Lord!')

Chapters 41–44:4: A vision of the Temple of the Lord, restored and renewed, with all the idolatrous practices that had defiled it removed and the building filled instead with the 'glory of the Lord' (44:4). Much of the rest of the book of Ezekiel concerns these future days of promise in a restored Jerusalem with the restored Temple as the centre of the worship of the Lord.

Daniel

This book relates in its opening six chapters several incidents from the years of Jewish captivity in Babylon in the first half of the sixth century BC, centred around Daniel, who is also known by his Babylonian name of Belteshazzar. These include the story of Daniel in the lions' den (chapter 3) and Daniel and his friends and the 'burning fiery furnace' (chapter 6). Both are seen as instances of God rewarding the courage and

faithfulness of his people to their own religion in an alien culture. In between these stories we read of Daniel's great wisdom and insight in the interpretation of the king's dreams, and also the story of Belshazzar's feast, at which the 'moving hand' wrote a message of judgment on the wall (chapter 5). All of these are certainly worth reading on many counts, but are probably not essential to a Reduced Bible.

One other unusual feature of the book of Daniel should be mentioned: it is the only one in the Bible that is written in two languages – most of it is written in Hebrew, as is the rest of the Old Testament, but chapters 2:4b–7:28 are written in Aramaic, the *lingua franca* of the ancient Near East, and the everyday language of Jesus and his friends. The book may be the work of different authors at different times, brought together at a later date.

Passages to read are all from the visions of Daniel, which occupy chapters 7 to the end.

To read
Chapter 7:9–14: The vision of the throne in heaven and an 'Ancient One' (literally 'Ancient of Days') who must be the Lord, sitting on it. A 'son of man' appears before the 'Ancient One' and is given dominion over every earthly power. This has always been assumed to have messianic

overtones. Jesus adopted the phrase 'Son of Man' as his own 'title' for himself. The prophecy comes in the middle of a vision of four beasts who were to terrorize the earth until conquered by the Ancient of Days.

Chapter 12:1–4: A time of anguish leading to a time of deliverance, in which even dead people will be raised to life – a concept not found in the earlier Hebrew Scriptures. Much of this language is echoed in the words of Jesus about the future (see, for instance, Mark 13:19–27).

Belshazzar's Feast by Rembrandt van Rijn (1606–69).

There now follow in the Bible twelve books, completing the Old Testament, which are known as the 'Minor Prophets', not because they are inferior or less important, but because they are much shorter than Isaiah, Jeremiah and Ezekiel, and even Daniel. It is probably only necessary (from the point of view of our Reduced Bible) to know a little about each by way of background. Where there are passages that are important either for what they say or for their part in the unfolding biblical story I have marked them below.

Hosea

The prophecies date from the eighth century BC. Hosea lived in the northern kingdom, Israel, which he sometimes calls 'Ephraim'. He warns his own people that their unfaithfulness – flirting with the Baal gods of their neighbouring tribes – would lead to God's judgment. As you will recognize by now, that's a pretty common theme of the prophets!

He illustrates this from his own personal experience, it would seem: his wife was unfaithful to him, but he later 'bought her back' for himself. The experts are divided as to whether this is autobiographical or simply illustrative, and in any case it doesn't much matter to the reader today.

To read

Chapter 1:2–10: The message of Hosea in summary: Israel had been unfaithful, but one day God would win her back to himself and unite her with the southern kingdom, Judah.

Chapter 6:1–10: The basic paradox of the book: God loves his people (v1–3) but their love for him is inconsistent and mostly empty show.

Chapter 11:1–11: A lovely poem of the love of God even in the face of his people's indifference.

Joel

A powerful piece of prophetic literature, not as concerned as most of the others with immediate political threats. It was possibly written in the fifth century BC. It uses a terrifying plague of locusts as its sign of judgment. Repentance is called for – not ritual, but real. Then the Spirit of God will be poured out (2:28–32) and God's enemies judged (chapter 3).

To read

Chapter 2:28–32: These are the best known words from Joel, quoted by the apostle Peter on the day of Pentecost (Acts 2:17–21).

Amos

The prophet Amos lived in the eighth century BC in the southern kingdom, Judah, but much of his message is directed at the people of Samaria, just to the north. Although privileged to share the Jewish religion, they had corrupted it and inevitably judgment will follow. The book includes five visions of judgment and also the obligatory passage near the end offering hope and restoration of David's throne at some future date.

To read

Chapter 3:2–8: To be chosen is to accept responsibility. Those to whom God has given most will be judged more harshly for their sins (for the rather gentler version of this in the teaching of Jesus see Luke 12:48). God is the ultimate master of our destiny and the prophets are his voice (6–7).

Chapter 8:4–7: A famous judgment on social and economic injustice.

Chapter 9:13–15: The inevitable hopeful ending, in a series of memorable images.

Obadiah

The shortest book in the Hebrew Scriptures – and parts of it can be found in Jeremiah and Joel. Obadiah was a contemporary of both. His message is of God's judgment on the people of Edom, because of the way they had treated Israel. There is no 'essential' reading here.

Jonah

Just about everyone knows the story of Jonah in the belly of the whale (literally, 'big fish'). The trouble is, that's about all they *do* know about this fascinating little book. The experts are more or less agreed that it doesn't set out to relate a strictly historical narrative, but instead is a kind of extended allegory on the themes of God's guidance, human repentance and gratitude for divine grace. Jonah is sent by God to warn the people of Nineveh – Gentiles, of course – to

turn from their sins or he will punish them. He is reluctant to go and do this, mostly, it would seem because he's not very fond of these foreigners! He tries to escape from God's call by taking a boat trip, but a storm hits the vessel, the sailors decide (on his own testimony) that it's Jonah's fault, and throw him overboard. Enter the big fish, and by the time Jonah emerges three days later from its belly he accepts that he'd better do what God requires. He preaches to the people of Nineveh – and they repent and are forgiven by God. Instead of being pleased, Jonah is annoyed that they've got off! However, sitting under the shade of a large bush, Jonah learns an important lesson about rejoicing at other people's blessings, even Gentiles.

To read
Chapters 3:10–4:11: Jonah's object lesson from God.

Micah

Micah is an ancient prophet with a remarkably 'modern' message – in fact, the average contemporary reader will probably find much in it with which to agree! He was more or less contemporary with Isaiah, though rather younger, and foretold judgment on Samaria and especially Jerusalem which at that point was some time in the future. However, his main complaint was not that the people had succumbed to the corrupting influences of Canaanite religion, but the much more fundamental sins of greed and exploitation of the poor and powerless. He sets out God's requirements in language of unequalled eloquence.

To read
Chapter 3:9–12: The sins of a 'religious' people.

*Chapter 4:1–5: A beautiful picture of the ideal society, living under the protection of God.

*Chapter 6:6–8: As precise a summary as the Bible offers of what true 'worship' entails.

Nahum
Nahum's prophecy is described as a 'vision' and probably dates from the seventh century BC, after the fall of Thebes, the great northern city of Egypt, but before the fall of Nineveh to the invading Medes. He sees these events as evidence of an immutable principle of the Lord, that those who set themselves up and claim the power and authority that is his alone will be brought down. In terms of a Reduced Bible, there is no essential reading here.

Habakkuk
Very little is known about the author and it is difficult even to put a date to the book. It is a fierce debate as to how it could be that a

holy God could use a people as corrupt as the Chaldeans to punish his own people, the resolution being that they too, in due course, will fall under his judgment. There is no required reading in this short book.

Zephaniah
Zephaniah (seventh century) repeats the warnings of earlier prophets to Judah and Jerusalem to repent before disaster strikes. However, his main emphasis is on the coming 'Day of the Lord', the moment when God would re-establish his just and gentle rule over both Israel and the nations. This was to become a major feature in Jewish thought right through to the time of Christ, who connected his own 'second coming' to this great day of God's justice – though without the terrible note of punishment and wrath that this prophet describes.

To read
Chapter 1:14–18: The Day of the Lord as the day of long overdue retribution for sin.

*Chapter 3:14–20: A very different picture of the same day – now a time of rejoicing and restoration. This follows the blessing of the 'remnant of Israel' (3:13) – faithful Jews through whom blessing will eventually come. This theme was also to become an important one in both Old and New Testament Scriptures.

Haggai

Haggai prophesied at the time of Nehemiah, eighteen years after the rebuilding of the Temple had begun and when the work (as it often can) seemed to have ground to a halt. His message is to consider how God has blessed them and to review their priorities. The house of God still lies in ruins, but their own houses are comfortable. No wonder the economy is falling apart! Put God first, and you will prosper, he tells them. Thus encouraged the 'remnant of the people' get back to work on the Temple (1:14,15).

To read

Chapter 2:6–9: the blessing that follows obedience.

Zechariah

Like Haggai, this book relates to the period of the rebuilding of Jerusalem. Chapters 1–8 refer to the events described in Ezra 5–6, in the later years of the sixth century BC.

The book relates eight visions, some very much in the apocalyptic (hidden) style, which are probably not to be tied to specific historical events. In the later chapters, which are probably a compilation of sayings from other prophets, there is reference to a 'Good Shepherd' of the people whose death would open a fountain that cleanses from sin and bring an end to the prophetic era (13:1–9).

To read

Chapter 8:1–8: A picture of a renewed Jerusalem, old people sticks in hands, children playing in the streets, all enjoying the blessings of God.

Chapter 12:10–14; 13:1; 7–9: The striking down of the Lord's servant/shepherd, and the blessing that will eventually flow from it. Traditionally, Christians have seen here prophecies about Jesus, the 'Good Shepherd' (John 10:11).

Malachi

The last book of the Old Testament, it was probably written in the fifth century BC. The Temple has been rebuilt, and not yet been destroyed by the invading Greeks. The sacrifices are being offered, but the priests are casual and careless in their religious observances. The people are content, but have compromised their religion by accepting mixed marriages and not paying their Temple tithes (offerings) in full. Various accusations along these lines are put to Israel by the prophet and he then counters their supposed replies. In chapter 3 we move on to the now prevalent idea of the 'Day of the Lord' which will bring both judgment and blessing.

To read

Chapter 3:1–5: The Day of the Lord as a time both of justice and blessing.

Chapter 4:1–6: The day when the 'sun of righteousness shall rise, with healing in its wings' (remember 'Hark the Herald Angels Sing'?). And 'Elijah' will come to prepare people's hearts for that day (see Luke 1:18, where this is referred to John the Baptist).

The Apocrypha

Some Bibles, usually those intended largely for a Roman Catholic readership, have six or seven books placed in the Old Testament section which do not normally appear in others, or have additional material in other books, particularly Esther and Daniel. This text (mostly originally recorded only in the Greek version of the Old Testament) makes up what is called the 'Apocrypha', from the Greek word 'hidden'. These books and material are sometimes called the 'Deutero-canonical Books' – books which fall into a second 'canon', or recognized list of writings. Their status within the Hebrew Scriptures was long debated. In Bibles used by Reformed and Protestant Churches this apocryphal material is sometimes included as a separate section, placed between the Old and New Testaments. The position of the Church of England, for instance, as set out in the Thirty-Nine Articles, is that these 'other books', as it calls them, 'the Church doth read for example of life and instruction of manners; but yet doth it not apply them to establish any doctrine'. In other words, the Apocrypha has valuable things to say about faith and behaviour, but is not to be given the same authority as the 'canonical Scriptures'. Their exact status has always been a matter of dispute, but in the sixteenth century the Roman Catholic Church officially placed them in its 'canon' and they have been from then on part of its Scriptures.

The New Testament

Matthew
We've already looked at the Gospels of Matthew, Mark, Luke and John in some detail, so for the purposes of our Reduced Bible I propose a few passages from each, representing the particular styles and approach of the four of them. However, even in the restrictions of a Reduced Bible it would easily be possible to include a complete reading of all the Gospels. After all, taken together they add up to no more than a slim paperback book.

To read
Chapter 2:1–15: Matthew's account of the birth of Jesus – a rather different story from Luke's, and from a very different angle.

The determining factor with Matthew, here as elsewhere, is readily seen to be the fulfilment of the Old Testament prophecies (see vv. 6 and 15). In fact there are several other allusions to the Scriptures hidden in his story.

Chapter 5:1–12: The famous 'Beatitudes' – the description of those who are 'blessed' by God.

Chapter 6:23–34: Words of Jesus about the worries of life.

Chapter 11:25–30: The invitation of Jesus to the 'weary'.

Chapter 13:1–9: The parable of the Sower – a typical instance of the teaching style of Jesus.

Chapter 14:13–21: Matthew's version of the feeding of the five thousand – rather fuller than Mark's.

Chapter 16:13–27: The turning point in the Gospels – the moment when the disciples confessed their belief that Jesus was indeed the Messiah. His reaction to it, which surprised them.

Chapter 18:1–5: Jesus on the nature of faith – child-like, but not childish.

Appearance on Mount Galilee by Duccio di Buoninsegna (c. 1260–1318).

Chapter 21:1–13: The triumphant entry into Jerusalem of Jesus 'the prophet from Galilee'. Jesus drives the traders out of the Temple.

Chapter 25:31–45: A parable of the judgment of the 'nations' – the people who have not been taught about the Lord. The 'sheep and the goats' – almost indistinguishable among the mountain flocks.

*Chapter 26:57–68: The trial of Jesus before the high priest.

(We shall follow Mark's account of the trial before Pilate, judgment and crucifixion of Jesus, supplemented by aspects of the story which the other Gospels elaborate. We shall follow Luke's account of the resurrection, on the same basis.)

*Chapter 28:16–20: The 'Great Commission' – Jesus sends out his disciples to carry his message to the whole world ('all nations') – and he promises to be with them for ever.

Mark

To read

Chapter 1:1–15: With his customary brevity, Mark carries us swiftly through the ministry of John the Baptist, 'preparing the way' for the Messiah, his baptism of Jesus and the dramatic arrival of Jesus in Galilee, 'proclaiming the good news of God'.

Chapter 2:1–12: Jesus not only heals a lame man, but forgives his sins, to general shock and horror!

Chapter 3:13–19: Jesus chooses his twelve 'apostles' (the word means 'messengers').

*Chapter 4:35–41: Jesus calms the storm.

Chapter 6:14–29: The execution by king Herod of John the Baptist, at the request of Herodias' daughter.

Chapter 7:1–23: Jesus distinguishes between religious traditions and rituals and true inner cleanliness.

*Chapter 9:1–13: The 'transfiguration' of Jesus – the disciples on the mountain have a vision of Jesus in his glory, with Moses the law-giver and Elijah, the first of the great prophets of Israel. God tells them to listen to *him*.

*Chapter 9:30–41: A solemn warning about what lay ahead. A lesson in true humility. And another on the danger of an 'exclusive' approach to religion.

Chapter 11:27–33: Questions about authority.

*Chapter 12:28–34: The greatest commandment.

Chapter 13:1–27: Jesus offers his own 'apocalypse' – a hidden or coded prophesy about what lay

DOCTOR LUKE

When we think of the biblical writers, Luke must take an important place. His two substantial books, the Gospel of Luke and the Acts of the Apostles, account for more than a quarter of the whole of the New Testament.

A consummate storyteller, Luke was also a careful and stylish writer. He was well educated, a 'physician', and a frequent companion of the apostle Paul on his travels. He was born in what we would now call Turkey, and first met Paul, it seems, at Antioch.

ahead until his return 'in great glory'.

Chapter 14:1–13: A woman anoints the feet of Jesus. Judas decides to betray him.

Chapter 14:17–50: The 'last supper', the agony in the Garden of Gethsemane and the arrest of Jesus by a crowd led by Judas Iscariot. The disciples flee.

Chapter 14:66–72: Peter denies Jesus.

Chapter 15: Mark's Passion account – the trial before Pilate, the release of the criminal Barabbas, the scourging, the crucifixion, death and burial in a private tomb.

Luke
To read
Chapter 1:26–38: The 'annunciation' – the angel tells Mary she will be the mother of the Messiah. The 'hail Mary' greeting.

Chapter 2:1–19: The birth of Jesus in Bethlehem.

Chapter 3:1–6: The beginning of the ministry of John the Baptist.

Chapter 4:1–13: The temptation (or 'testing') of Jesus in the wilderness.

Chapter 4:16–30: Jesus in the synagogue of his hometown, Nazareth.

Chapter 7:18–23: John's disciples ask Jesus whether he is the 'one who is to come'. His answer – look at the evidence!

Chapter 7:36–49: A 'sinful woman' anoints the feet of Jesus.

Chapter 10:25–37: The Good Samaritan – the true 'neighbour'.

Chapter 11:1–4: The Lord's prayer (see also Matthew 6:9–13 for a longer version).

Chapter 14:1–11: A healing on the Sabbath (one of several). The

The Bible Made Clear

nature of true honour, which cannot be 'claimed'.

Chapter 15:11–32: The story of the Prodigal Son and his elder brother. The value to the 'father' of the one who was lost.

Chapter 18:9–14: The Pharisee and the tax-collector – a lesson in true repentance.

Chapter 20:27–29: Jesus refutes the Sadducees on the question of the resurrection of the dead.

Chapter 23:32–43: Jesus, on the cross, forgives his killers, and also a penitent thief being crucified alongside him.

Chapter 24:1–43: Luke's account of the resurrection appearances of Jesus – to the women, first; then to two of his followers on the road home to Emmaus; finally to all the disciples in the upper room in Jerusalem.

Chapter 24:50–53: Jesus leaves his disciples and returns to heaven.

John

John's Gospel, as we have seen, is different in style, approach and in some respects content from the other three. What I suggest for the Reduced Bible are a few of the distinctive and significant passages in John which reflect that difference.

LEFT: *Jesus Alone on the Cross* by James Tissot (1836–1902).

To read

Chapter 1:1–18: The magnificent 'prologue' to John's Gospel – reflecting the opening verse of Genesis ('In the beginning, God...') and introducing the concept of Jesus as God's 'Word' – his 'explanation', the key to understanding.

Chapter 2:1–11: The 'water into wine' – the first 'sign' of Christ's 'glory'.

Chapter 3:1–17: The dialogue between Jesus and Nicodemus, a leader of the Jews and member of the Council.

Chapter 4:19–24: The true nature of worship – explained to a Samaritan woman at the well of Jacob.

Chapter 5:19–29: Jesus explains to a critical audience the nature of his own mission on earth – to give 'life'.

Chapter 6:30–51: Following the miracle of the loaves and fishes, Jesus explains to the crowd who have followed him that he is the true 'bread of life'.

Chapter 8:1–11: The woman caught in the act of adultery.

Chapter 8:31–36: The nature of true freedom.

Chapter 10:1–16: Jesus the 'good shepherd'.

Chapter 11:1–44: The raising of Lazarus.

JESUS

Oddly enough, although the religion which bears his name offers its followers a great deal of wonderful teaching given by Jesus, as far as we know he never wrote a book himself. The only reference to Jesus writing anything in the New Testament is some words he scribbled in the dust when the crowd of men pushed a woman accused of adultery before him (John 8:6).

Nevertheless we have in the four Gospels many passages of teaching that are ascribed to him. Those in Matthew, Mark and Luke are couched in the style of a Jewish teacher of the time; those recorded by John are rather different both in style and content, perhaps reflecting an elderly disciple's recall of the impression the words of Jesus made on his first hearers.

There seems no reason to doubt that what we have in the Gospels is an authentic reflection of the teaching of Jesus. Certainly it's hard to believe that any ordinary mortal could have invented it!

Chapter 13:1–17: Jesus washes his disciples' feet.

Chapter 14:1–17: Jesus as the way, the truth and the life, the perfect 'image' of the Father. The promise of the coming of the Holy Spirit, the 'Advocate' or Helper of his people.

Chapter 15:12–17: The new commandment of Jesus.

Chapter 18:28–40: Pilate's examination of Jesus (a longer version than that in the other Gospels).

Chapter 19:29–30: Jesus arranges for his mother's care. He dies.

Chapter 20:11–18: Jesus and Mary Magdalene in the garden of the resurrection.

Chapter 21:13–19: Peter is cross-examined by Jesus and then re-commissioned.

Acts

Acts is Luke's account of the early years of the Christian church, in the days of the apostles. As a companion of Paul, he was an eye-witness of some events later in the story. The passages chosen are those I suggest are more significant, but the whole story is fascinating.

To read:
Chapter 1:6–12: The 'ascension' of Jesus to heaven.

Chapter 2:1–42: The day of Pentecost (Whitsun). The pouring out of the Holy Spirit upon the apostles. Peter's sermon and a mass baptism!

Chapter 7:51–60: The martyrdom of Stephen, following a powerful speech to the Council – only the last part of it is included in this reading.

*Chapter 9:1–19: The conversion of Saul (Paul) on the road to Damascus.

*Chapter 10: The conversion and baptism of Cornelius and his household, the first gentile converts to Christianity.

Chapter 12:1–11: James (the leader of the Jerusalem church) is executed and Peter imprisoned, but released by an angel.

Chapter 13:1–12: Saul (Paul) and others are commissioned for what we would now call 'missionary work'.

The remainder of the Acts of the Apostles is a detailed account of Paul's journeys to preach and to establish churches all over Asia Minor and then Greece. It ends with his hazardous journey to Rome as a prisoner, to plead his case before the emperor, and house arrest in the city.

Romans

When we turn to the letters of the apostle Paul it is necessary to take a rather different approach. I have tried to summarize the main argument of each of them, and

PAUL

The apostle Paul was born in the Jewish community of a town in Asia Minor (Turkey), called Tarsus. Educated as an orthodox Jew, his conversion on the Damascus Road is one of the great turning points of Christian history. His letters to the various Christian churches he had either founded or supported take up almost a quarter of the New Testament, though some modern scholars have disputed whether he was the actual author of some of them. In any case, following the practice of the day, he employed a scribe, who may at times have reproduced the apostle's ideas in his own words. In terms of actual words written by Paul, we have a mere handful – occasions when he says that he has added this in his own hand, perhaps to authenticate the authority of the message (see, for instance, 1 Corinthians 16:21, Galatians 6:11).

Most of Paul's letters can be dated between AD 54 and 60, about twenty-four to thirty years after the death of Jesus, and twenty to twenty-six years after his Damascus Road experience.

then to follow that with one, two or at most a few brief 'tasters' of the contents. Paul is quite a subtle arguer, and I admit that much of that subtlety will be lost by this method. However, I hope the experience will whet your appetite to tackle the whole meal one day!

Romans is Paul's great work of theology, in which he sets out his case that the way to God is not through the keeping of rules and regulations (what he calls 'the Law') but by faith in Jesus Christ as a gift of God (what he calls 'grace'). He demonstrates that this principle has always applied, in that faith was at the heart of the relationship between the great figures of Israel's past and the Lord. As in all the letters, he ends with practical advice about lifestyle and worship, and with personal greetings.

To read

Chapter 1:1–4: A summary of the gospel that Paul serves.

Chapter 1:18–23: The nature of the world without faith in God.

Chapter 3:21–26: Paul's case in brief – all have sinned, all can be 'justified' (counted as guiltless) by God's grace through what Jesus has done for us.

Chapter 8:31–39: A moving testimony to Paul's conviction that nothing on earth or in heaven can ever separate us from God's love for us in Christ.

Chapters 9–11: The question of the future of the Jewish people, the heirs of the original covenant. It would seem that his belief was that finally 'all Israel would be saved' (11:26).

Chapter 12:9–21: How Christians ought to live – echoes here of the teaching of Jesus.

1 Corinthians

The two letters to the church at Corinth are clearly responses, first to reports that have reached Paul, and then to a letter he had received from them. The first letter deals with matters of church discipline and worship (a serious case of sexual sin, and an undisciplined use of the charismatic gift of tongues). However, the book includes one or two memorable passages, which are noted below.

To read

Chapter 1:18–25: The 'folly' of the cross compared to the wisdom of human 'philosophy' (learning).

Chapter 11:23–29: The earliest record we have of the institution of the Holy Communion by Jesus (around AD 55).

Chapter 13: Paul's famous hymn to love (*agape* – self-giving, sacrificial love).

Chapter 15:11: Paul's summary of the Christian gospel as he was taught it after his conversion. Again, probably the earliest written record of the resurrection events.

2 Corinthians
A letter re-asserting Paul's authority as an apostle, over against some unnamed detractors at Corinth.

To read

Chapter 4:5–12: How Paul saw the apostolic ministry – servants, not masters.

Chapter 12:1–10: Paul's wonderful visions, and his 'thorn in the flesh'.

Galatians
An angry letter to a church which, Paul felt, was being led astray by people who wanted to draw them back into the letter of the Jewish law.

To read

Chapter 2:19–21: Paul's personal testimony.

*Chapter 5:13–26: The use and abuse of true freedom. The contrast between life dictated by our lower nature ('the flesh') and life in the Spirit.

Ephesians
To read

Chapters 5:21–6:20: How a Christian household should conduct itself (first century

model!), and the source of spiritual strength (prayer, truth, righteousness).

Philippians
Possibly Paul's favourite church! (You can read how it was started in Acts 16:11–40.) Many women are mentioned in its leadership.

To read

*Chapter 2:5–12: The self-emptying of Jesus and his exaltation by God as a model for Christian humility.

*Chapter 4:4–9: A well-known passage – how to find both the peace of God and the God of peace.

Colossians
A letter to a church Paul had not visited.

To read

Chapter 1:15–20: Paul's understanding of the place of Jesus Christ in the divine order of things – the one through whom the whole creation, no less, would be reconciled to God.

1 Thessalonians
The two letters to the church at Thessalonica are written to correct their misgivings about fellow-Christians who had died, and also about the second coming of Christ (which the early church expected imminently).

To read:

Chapter 4:13–18: The place of the Christian dead, and of those who are alive at the second coming.

Chapter 5:1–11: The certainty of the return of Jesus, at an unknown time and date.

2 Thessalonians
To read:

Chapter 2:1–5: A further assertion of the certainty of Christ's coming, but not, apparently, until 'the lawless one' will have appeared and tried to usurp God's place and temple (probably a reference to imperial Rome).

1 Timothy

The two letters to Timothy and the short one to Titus are clearly different from Paul's other letters in that they are addressed to familiar individuals rather than to churches. Timothy and Titus are obviously regarded by the apostle as younger men who will continue his mission after his (apparently imminent) death, and also guard the church from going off the rails. These are rather different pre-occupations from those of the other letters, and may account for their very different tone, style and even vocabulary. Experts agree that it is difficult, if not impossible, to put these letters into any kind of historical context, as Paul's movements after those recorded

in Acts are unknown, as is his eventual fate, though it is assumed that he was martyred.

To read:

Chapter 2:1–7: Priorities in prayer.

Chapter 6:11–16: An exhortation to Timothy to live a life appropriate for a minister of God.

2 Timothy
To read:

Chapter 4:1–8: A last commission of Timothy, and a final message of faith from Paul.

Titus

A short letter to Titus, an earlier convert of Paul's, who is now charged with responsibility for the churches in Crete, including the selection and appointment of ministers and the maintenance of sound doctrine and a Christian lifestyle. There is nothing here that is essential to our Reduced Bible, but the following passages may be found interesting: 1:15; 2:11–13; 3:4–7.

Philemon

Another 'solo' letter of Paul's – this time to a slave owner whose slave has run away and has recently been serving Paul during a time of home imprisonment. It's an interesting insight into the moral conflict slavery created for first-century Christians – Paul is

sending him back to his (Christian) owner, but not, he says, as a slave, but as a 'beloved brother'. It's a short letter and probably worth reading for the light it sheds on the contemporary view of slavery.

Hebrews

This is a letter from an anonymous author written to Jewish Christians. It sets out in some detail the relationship between the two covenants. It also contains several warnings to its readers not to revert to Judaism. For our immediate purposes, it contains a number of passages which certainly help to clarify how the Christians saw their faith as built on the foundation of the revelation given originally to the patriarchs and prophets of Israel.

To read:
Chapter 1:1–14: Christ is superior to the angels and to the ancient prophets of Israel, because he is God's Son.

Chapter 10:1–14: The Law as a 'shadow' of the 'good things to come' in Christ, who is a priest who by a single and unrepeated offering has taken sins away for ever.

Chapter 11:1–3: A helpful, short definition of faith!

Chapter 12:1–2: The Christian's priority – 'looking to Jesus'.

A Jewish scribe at work.

James

A short book of instruction by James, who calls himself simply 'a servant of God and of the Lord Jesus Christ' but was probably the 'bishop' (or leader) of the early church in Jerusalem and is widely identified with the brother (or step-brother) of Jesus (see Mark 6:3). It has many echoes of Jesus' Sermon on the Mount, is strongly Jewish in its background and is very practical and down to earth.

To read:

Chapter 1:22–27: A practical, effective religion.

Chapter 4:5–18: The dangers of an uncontrolled tongue, and the blessings of a peaceful lifestyle.

Chapter 4:1–10: Avoiding conflict – submitting to God.

1 Peter

The first of two letters ascribed to the apostle Peter and addressed to Christians dispersed across the Near East – presumably scattered following the first waves of persecution of the church, which are referred to in the text.

To read:

Chapter 1:3–9: A moving expression of gratitude to the Father of 'our Lord Jesus Christ'.

Chapter 2:4–10: The church as the new 'Israel', God's 'royal priesthood'.

2 Peter

A letter from a very late part of the apostolic period – Peter's authorship has often been challenged. It deals with a time when questions are being asked about the long delay in the second coming of Christ (3:3–10).

To read:

Chapter 1:16–21: A recollection of the transfiguration and an endorsement of the authority of scripture (though not 'a matter of one's own interpretation'!).

1 John

The first of three short letters by John, the author of the fourth Gospel. He is writing to churches he knows or has founded, warning them against false teaching (especially about the nature of Jesus) and encouraging them in their faith.

To read:

Chapter 1:1–2:2: The heart of the apostolic message – and a realistic view about sin and forgiveness.

Chapter 4:7–21: A classic passage on the nature of God, who is love, and therefore the requirement that we should love each other.

2 & 3 John

Letters, apparently to a Christian woman of influence, urging her to reject false teachers and their teaching. There is no 'obligatory' reading here.

Jude

A short letter by Jude, mostly concerned, once again, with combating heresy and division in the church.

Revelation

This strange but fascinating book was discussed at length in the section on 'the Bible and the Future'. Now it's time to include some of its more memorable visions and images in our Reduced Bible.

To read:

Chapter 1:9–20: John describes how these visions came to him while he was 'in the spirit' on a Sunday ('the Lord's day), on the island of Patmos where he was in exile. The first vision is of the risen Christ in glory and of the messages he has for the seven churches of Asia Minor (modern Turkey). These follow in chapters 2 and 3.

Chapter 5:1–14: A vision of heaven – the throne of God and the Lamb 'as if it had been slaughtered' (Jesus). The scroll with seven seals (hidden knowledge), to be revealed as the seals are broken.

Chapter 7:9–17: The glory of the martyrs in heaven, their robes washed white 'in the blood of the Lamb'.

Chapters 8–18: Various plagues and judgments that will afflict the earth, including the downfall of 'Babylon the Great' (obviously imperial Rome) presided over by a 'beast' with seven heads and ten horns. Throughout it all God and the Lamb are seen presiding over the whole enterprise, indeed, orchestrating it.

Chapter 19:1–21: At last God intervenes directly, his army clothed in fine linen, pure and white, led by a white horse called 'Faithful and True', wreaking judgment on the evil-doers.

Chapter 20:1–15: The devil and his servants are bound and rendered powerless. The 'great white throne' of God's judgment day.

Chapter 21:1–7: The New Jerusalem.

Chapter 21:22–22:13: The glory of heaven. The nations healed. 'Nothing will be accursed any more.' Christ – now called 'Alpha and Omega', divine titles – will come soon.

Final Word

You have now completed the Reduced Bible! If you have followed it through and taken up all the readings, you will have a reasonably complete picture of the message of the Bible, which I hope will whet your appetite to explore more completely this amazing compilation, beyond question the most influential book in the history of our civilization.

We began with its 'plot', and perhaps that is the correct place to end. The Bible is not a 'literary masterpiece' (though in the King James Version, couched in elegant Tudor English, it undoubtedly is). It is not primarily a scientific manual, nor a source of historical or geographical information (though obviously it does provide both, from time to time). It is not a collection of stories or an anthology of poetry (though there are marvellous stories and beautiful poems within its pages). This, from countless hands and diverse minds, woven by an invisible but, I believe, divine skill over many centuries, claims to be no less than 'the Word of God' – his message through the ages, his truth for every age. It would be a tragedy to have it in our hands and not even bother to investigate the claim.

Index

Picture Acknowledgments

p. 2 Elio Ciol/Corbis; p. 9 The Gallery Collection/Corbis; p. 10 Israelimages.com/Karen Benzian; p. 13 Hanan Isachar/Alamy; pp. 16–17 Jim Zuckerman/Corbis; p. 18 INTERFOTO Pressebildagentur/Alamy; p. 22 Zev Radovan/www.BibleLandPictures.com; p. 29 Burstein Collection/Corbis; p. 31 Corbis; p. 34 Hanan Isachar/Holylandimages.com; pp. 38–39 Suk-Heui Park/ Photographer's Choice/Getty Images Ltd; p. 43 Massimo Listri/Corbis; p. 46 Skyscan/Corbis; p. 50 © Photo SCALA, Florence 1990 – courtesy of the Ministero Beni e Att. Culturali; p. 54 Dean Conger/Corbis; p. 58 Janet Jarman/Corbis; p. 59 Janet Jarman/Corbis; p. 61 Hanan Isachar/Holylandimages.com; p. 69 Hanan Isachar/Holylandimages.com; p. 72 Hanan Isachar/Holylandimages.com; p. 76 Visual Arts Library (London)/Alamy; p. 79 Alinari Archives/Corbis; p. 82 © Photo SCALA, Florence 1990. Paris, Louvre; p. 84 Michael & Patricia Fogden/Corbis; pp. 88–89 Elio Ciol/Corbis; p. 94 Jon Arnold/ Jonarnoldimages.com; p. 105 Hanan Isachar/Holylandimages.com; pp. 106–107 Yann Arthus-Bertrand/Corbis; p. 114 Lion Hudson; p. 119 Zev Radovan/www.BibleLandPictures.com; p. 124 Visual Arts Library (London)/Alamy; p. 127 Archivo Iconografico, S.A./Corbis; p. 130 David Alexander; p. 132 © Photo SCALA, Florence 1990; p. 137 National Gallery Collection; By kind permission of the Trustees of the National Gallery, London/Corbis; p. 143 © Photo SCALA, Florence 1990. Photo Opera Metropolitana Siena/Scala, Florence; p. 146 Brooklyn Museum/Corbis; p. 153 Richard Nowitz/Israelimages.com.